FINDING THE FOX

A red fox in a zoo seeks out contact with visitors.
Langedrag Nature Park, Norway, February.

ANDREAS TJERNSHAUGEN

TRANSLATED BY LUCY MOFFATT

Finding the
FOX

ENCOUNTERS WITH
AN ENIGMATIC ANIMAL

GREYSTONE BOOKS

Vancouver/Berkeley/London

Greystone Books Ltd.
greystonebooks.com

Cataloguing data available from Library and Archives Canada
ISBN 978-1-77840-072-8 (cloth)
ISBN 978-1-77840-073-5 (epub)

Editing for English edition by James Penco
Proofreading by Alison Strobel
Scientific review by Mark Statham
Cover and text design by Jessica Sullivan
Cover illustrations by Elena Malgina/Dreamstime
and Lilithcollageart/Creative Market
Interior photographs by Andreas Tjernshaugen,
except where credited otherwise

Printed and bound in Canada on FSC® certified paper at Friesens. The FSC® label
means that materials used for the product have been responsibly sourced.

Greystone Books thanks the Canada Council for the Arts, the British Columbia
Arts Council, the Province of British Columbia through the Book Publishing Tax
Credit, and the Government of Canada for supporting our publishing activities.

This translation has been published with the financial support of NORLA.

Greystone Books gratefully acknowledges the xʷməθkʷəy̓əm (Musqueam),
Sḵwx̱wú7mesh (Squamish), and səl̓ílwətaʔɬ (Tsleil-Waututh) peoples on
whose land our Vancouver head office is located.

"It is quite mad to believe that the fox has put aside its wild skin and its wild nature, to stand in the church and sing like some kind of nun."

HERMAN WEIGERE
A Fox Book, 1555

Contents

The Den

THE FOX'S DEN is just a stone's throw from the forest trail, but it is unlikely that many of those passing by in boots or runners are aware of it. To find the den, you have to clamber or slide three or four yards down a soil slope, then deal with the next obstacle—the stream. In dry periods, I simply jump over it or walk across from stone to stone, but when it is swollen, I cross by balancing on an uprooted tree trunk. The fox does the same thing; I've seen its tracks in the new snow.

The slope down from the path forms one wall of a small ravine. On the other side, you can climb up yet another slope of loose soil to the end of a grainfield. Between the forest and the field, the ravine is like a secret room and the stream flattens out its dark floor—overgrown with ferns—when it breaks its banks and deposits the soil that it has carved out higher up. Or *streams*, to be more accurate. Down here, two streams merge into one, and farther up, between their two courses, towers the bank of earth that the fox has hollowed out and made its own. More than ten entrances to the den have been dug out across the top of the bank, some as much as half a yard wide. All may well be linked to one and the same tunnel system.

In old tales, the fox's subterranean home becomes a fortress, where sly Reynard the Fox—or Mikkel Rev, as he is known in Scandinavia, where I live—secures himself many exits and escape routes to ensure that he can always slip away if an enemy intrudes. In fact, this den system is largely the work of the vixen. Generations of fox mothers have dug out tunnels and breeding chambers here while the cubs were growing in their bellies. In the pitch darkness some yards into the bank of earth, they have given birth and suckled— if not every spring, at any rate often—for more than half a century.

In the winter, fox tracks and urine marks are visible in the snow beside the entrances. In spring, while the cubs are small, the mother maintains discipline, avoiding food spillage and an overly intense scent around the den so as not to reveal where this year's litter of cubs is hidden. Over the early summer, the cubs grow and start to peep outside, and that's when the chaos starts, as food scraps and playthings the parents have brought back for their young begin to pile up in the area around the den. One summer, I found feathers and bones here, as well as plastic packaging. "Whole wheat bread," it said on one of the plastic bags. "Organic figs" on another.

But even if you find a den as splendid as this one, with such a glorious history, don't imagine that you know where the fox is. Apart from a few weeks during breeding season, it sleeps sometimes here, sometimes there. When the birth draws near, the vixen chooses a den—perhaps she'll use the big old one this year, or perhaps another smaller one, or perhaps she'll choose to dig a totally new one. You may find signs that she has dug and prepared several places, either as a trial run or simply to confuse anyone who is on her trail. And you may pick up the acrid smell of fresh fox urine beside the entrance to a den where there is no litter of cubs on the way. Because that's what foxes are like— you never know what they're up to.

On the Trail

WE CLAMBER UP through the blueberry bushes. Topsy
has picked up a scent—flattening herself against the
ground, she hauls on the leash, and I have no objec-
tion as long as she's pulling me uphill. It's amazing
how much strength there is in a twenty-pound dog. A
pine root serves first as a handhold, then as a foothold, and after that I'm over the edge too. Before us,
an unfamiliar path comes into view, and Topsy is quite
determined that we should follow it to the left. I follow
her lead. Since it has been so difficult to catch more
than a brief glimpse of the fox until now, I have instead
set myself the task of finding as many traces of it as
possible, and today I've decided to see whether Topsy
can help. It's hard to say whether what she's scenting
now is a fox, or perhaps a marten—or, for that matter,
another person with a dog on a leash—but she knows
so much more than me about the routes animals have
taken across the forest floor that following her must
be worth a try.

TOPSY IS A Danish-Swedish farmdog. Her ears can't
quite decide whether to be erect or floppy, and many

people mistake her for a smooth-coated, long-legged Jack Russell. Farmdogs have traditionally earned their keep as mouse and rat hunters on the farms of southern Sweden and Denmark, and my own experience is that Topsy is keen to chase most things furred and feathered. As far as I know, she has only one extremely imprudent bullfinch on her conscience. The first time Topsy saw geese, she immediately crouched down and started to sneak toward them; we've stopped letting her off the leash in the forest at home after a few disappearing tricks—including the time she caught the scent of a roe deer and drove it across the hiking trail, right in front of us and a couple of other astonished families out on their Sunday walk.

Only once has Topsy been close to a fox. It came upon us unexpectedly as it was crossing the gravel track where we were taking an evening walk, and the dog became totally frantic the way she does when we pass a cat—she whimpered and lay flat against the ground, tugging on the leash. The encounter with the fox was exciting for me too. I had only seen red foxes on a handful of occasions. Even though I spent a lot of time on the lookout for wild animals when I was growing up, the only encounter with a fox that I recall from childhood is the time a seedy-looking specimen appeared in broad daylight on one of the small roads in my neighborhood. The mangy fox was covered in big bald patches. It stopped and looked at me with narrowed eyes from a distance of a few yards before slinking over to the verge of the road and vanishing among the trees. The reason there was barely a fox to be seen back then was an outbreak of sarcoptic mange; the mange epidemic of the 1970s and 1980s led to a collapse in the Norwegian fox population. Perhaps you might call it an attempt to make up for that childhood loss, this determination of mine to get to know the fox in my adulthood.

Because of this preoccupation with thoughts of foxes, I have also begun to take a renewed interest in our family dog. Topsy probably lives in a similar sensory world to her russet relative with the white-tipped tail; she certainly perceives the world differently from me. Whenever we find ourselves in a place where lots of other people walk their dogs, she'll sometimes spend a minute sniffing around, running her nose the length of every blade of grass or twig, probably to pick up as much detail as possible about the dogs that have urinated there. Sometimes Topsy will go out of her mind with excitement about something I can't see, but just as often I'll be the one who makes eye contact with a cat or a roe deer just a few yards off, which Topsy has failed to notice because the wind's blowing in the wrong direction. I imagine it must be roughly the same with foxes.

THE FOREST TRAIL Topsy and I have found turns out to be an animal track that simply peters out and vanishes, but she continues with her nose to the ground.

We come over a hilltop, then the terrain starts to slope downward. The open pine forest gives way to hazel trees, each with multiple thin stems that grow together at first, then shoot off in all directions. In the spring, the foliage on these fountains of wood casts so much shade that almost nothing can grow beneath them. The forest floor is strewn with brown leaves. It strikes me that this slope would be a good spot for a fox's den and, as Topsy drags me out into the clearing between a pine tree and a smooth rock, there, indeed, is a fox's lair. She sticks her nose into a hole that has obviously been dug out in the soil slope. A little farther off, there's another. Topsy is eager now and seems keen to head into the tunnels and explore the inside of the den, but I hold the leash taut because I don't want to risk the possibility of her getting stuck deep underground—or ending up in a scuffle with a fox or some other wild animal down there.

FOX'S DENS ARE generally located near a stream or other source of drinking water. But the tunnels mustn't get flooded, so there is little point searching all the way down by the course of the stream or out on the bog. The fox needs well-drained soil that is loose enough for easy excavation and deep enough for the den to extend several yards inward and downward. Slopes and inclines are promising places, and it is said that foxes prefer to dig in southern slopes. Rocky crevices, gaps beneath stumps and tree roots, talus slopes, and openings beneath buildings can also be used as the starting point for a den, and in places like these, it can be more difficult to distinguish the entrance of a den from a perfectly ordinary hole. In my neck of the woods, the fox prefers not to be seen by people. That's why it establishes its den in inaccessible or sheltered places, although these may be surprisingly close to houses, fields, or paths—because we humans are creatures of habit too, and even in landscapes that many people pass through, there are places where they rarely think of going.

Now and then the fox will move into an old badger's sett.* Over the years, the two species may take turns to inhabit the same tunnels, and in large, old den systems, they may even come to an arrangement whereby each uses its own end. The fox is only a cave dweller during the breeding season in spring. During the rest of the year, it may seek shelter in a den when the weather is poor or it is being pursued by enemies. Otherwise, the fox prefers to sleep beneath the open sky. The badger, on the other hand, lives in its sett all year round, and since it is a permanent residence, the paths leading in and out of the badger's sett are clearly trampled. The piles of earth left by the badger's endless digging are also much larger than those outside a

---

* The badgers in Norway are European badgers, *Meles meles*, the same species that occurs in the British Isles and on the continent of Europe. Their burrows are commonly called "setts." The species is not very closely related to the American badger, *Taxidea taxus*.

fox's den. In addition, the badger likes to fit out its sett with a soft underlay of materials like leaves and moss, which it replaces regularly, and you can often see signs that a badger is busy kicking out old den material or bringing in new. Yet the best evidence of a badger's sett is a distinct trench or ditch leading away from the entrance—the result of the badger's constant excavation work. The fox doesn't make such trenches. At an active fox's den, you will often smell the characteristic odor of fox, or you may see scraps of food around the entrance, which is unusual outside a badger's sett.

EVEN IF YOU CAN'T catch sight of a fox, you might be able to find traces of it. Where it has captured a bird, you'll often find a lot of feathers on the ground, some with their shafts bitten through by the sharp carnassial teeth some way back in the fox's mouth. If the bitten-off feathers are dispersed individually over a large area, this may mean that a litter of cubs has been rampaging around with the remains of the bird's carcass. However, if you find a collection of feathers that have all been meticulously plucked out with their shafts intact, it's more likely that a hawk, a falcon, or an owl has been there, stripping its prey. The fox often leaves its excrement pointedly on display, on a stump or an uprooted tree trunk, for example. The droppings are a little over half an inch thick and two to four inches long. They may be in several sections, bound together by hair from the fox's prey, and they are often twisted into a spiral form with a point at one end. In addition to hair, they often contain small mouse bones. Old fox dung becomes a whitish color. When it is fresh, it may be black or gray. Don't touch the excrement—it can contain pathogens. The smell will be the telltale sign of fresh fox dung or urine for anyone who has previously smelled a fox. It is unlike any scent left behind by dogs, cats, or other animals common in this part of the world. Possibly the best comparison I have come across is that it's similar to the smell of a newly opened jar of instant coffee, although this is a more animal odor that you simply have to familiarize yourself with.

The fox's pawprints are similar to those of a small- to medium-sized dog. You'll see the impression of a heel pad at the back and four toes with claw marks at the front. They are easy to distinguish from cats' pawprints, which lack the claw marks, and from those of badgers, which have five toes rather than four. Dogs and foxes are a bit more difficult to tell apart. The fox's pawprint is more elongated than a typical dog's—roughly two to three inches long and a good one-and-a-half inches wide. You can find out for sure if the pawprints belong to a fox if they're unusually sharp and clear—in fresh snow or wet sand, for example. If you then draw a horizontal line directly behind the two innermost front toes in a fox's pawprint, the two outer toes will lie fully behind the line. If you do the same with a dog's pawprint or with wolf tracks, the line will cut through the impression of the two outer toes.

ON A DAY when the sun glitters on fresh snow, we find fox tracks out in the field. At last, Topsy and I are both on the trail. She sniffs. I look. If the dog shows any sign of taking off after the tracks of boots and large dog's paws, I simply say, "Look!" Then Topsy lifts her head and widens her eyes. When I point in the direction the fox has gone, she understands what I want and runs onward along the fox's trail, nose to the ground. She likes this game. So do I.

At first the trail follows the edge of the forest, then it vanishes into an impenetrable coppice of young spruces where we lose it, but luckily the pawprints come into view again some yards off and cut straight across the field, with some detours around the midfield islets—those small rocky outcrops that tend to dot Scandinavian meadows and fields. The fox does not seem to have found any prey. Here and there, it has picked up speed and pounced as much as a couple of yards forward, but in the spot where it landed, there is no sign that anything happened—other than that it hurried on in the same direction. I hold Topsy back to prevent her tracks from obscuring those of the fox and kneel down to examine the pawprints in the snow. The sun has melted them, making them a little indistinct. Even so, I'm *almost* certain that these are fox prints and not the pawprints of some happy dog let off the leash. Later, we come across fresh tracks in a woodland glen where livestock graze in the summertime. The tracks meander across the meadow and lead me to a better spot for crossing the stream than the one I knew of already, and here I also find first-class evidence: urine in the snow. I look around me before getting down on all fours and lowering my nose toward the yellowish-brown patch, roughly the way Topsy does. I sniff. It smells of fox.

Like Cats and Dogs

IF YOU LOOK into the amber eyes of the fox, you'll discover that the pupils are vertical slits, like those of a cat. That's a clue about the nature of the fox right there—a cat's eyes in a slender canine body. The red fox is a relative of the dog and the wolf but is adapted to a somewhat catlike lifestyle because, like house cats—and the wildcats they are descended from—the fox is a lonely hunter. It seeks out small prey that it can capture by itself.

Hunting small rodents, like voles and mice, is something of a specialty for the fox. The mere sound of rustling and rummaging is enough to tell it precisely where they are, even beneath snow or in long grass. To avoid alerting its prey before it is too late, the fox is careful to approach on soundless feet. For the last stretch, it flies through the air. The fox crouches down, then leaps high and forward in the air usually by about a yard—though up to five, if necessary—adjusting its course along the way with its long tail and landing right on top of the rodent, trapping it either in its jaws or beneath a paw. The red fox is a skilled hunter then, yet it is utterly incapable of the kind of teamwork we see when a pack of wolves work together to bring down a great moose that none of them could have defeated single-handed. If the hunt is successful, the fox eats alone. With a mouse, there really isn't much to share anyway.

The fox's body is designed for the great leaps: It is light. Its skeleton is delicate. Every single bone is simply thinner and weighs less than one might expect in a mammal of its size. The long winter coat that keeps the fox warm in northern climes may make it look nice and plump, but in the summer the slenderness of its body becomes apparent. The fox's body lacks the deep rib cage typical of a dog. Its internal organs are lighter, because one of the features that makes the fox so lightly built is a smaller stomach. Whereas the wolf can eat as much as 20 percent of its own body weight, a fox can barely manage more than 10 percent—so while the wolf can survive for a long time on a single meal, the fox must eat at regular intervals. Instead of storing food in its belly like the wolf, it buries supplies— little morsels all over the place, a single mouse, say—if it has anything left over.

A typical Scandinavian red fox is around sixteen inches high to the shoulder—a bit bigger than the typical red fox found in Britain or North America. Without its long, bushy tail, its body is twenty-four to thirty-three inches long, but the fox usually weighs only nine to eighteen pounds. If I check Topsy with a measuring tape and put her on the bathroom scale—which she submits to reluctantly and only when bribed with treats—she is shorter than a fully grown fox and roughly as long, but heavier than most foxes. Even though her forebears have lived with people for millennia and have certainly caught mice and rats on Danish and Swedish farms for many generations, her lupine heritage is reflected in her build. She also subjects her toys to the method the wolf uses to kill any small prey: she picks the toy up in her jaws and shakes it hard. The fox doesn't use that method. It sinks its long, sharp canine teeth into its prey and bites down hard until it's dead, repeatedly if necessary—roughly the way a cat does.

The fox has some other feline traits. For example, it will often stand side-on and arch its back when engaged in conflict. And then there are its eyes. Pupils shaped like vertical slits occur mainly in predators that hunt after dark. This eye construction is apparently helpful for judging distances accurately in poor light and is most common among predators that rely on taking their prey by surprise, like cats and foxes, rather than by pursuing it openly over long distances, the way wolves do. The fox's gaze reveals it to be a stealthy hunter and night wanderer.

ALTHOUGH THE FOX's hunting behavior may be reminiscent of the cat's, their diets are different. The cat is almost exclusively carnivorous. The fox, on the other hand, eats almost anything. It is, for example, fond of fruits and berries—just like Topsy, who throws herself heart and soul into blueberrying, helping herself directly from the bushes and happily performing tricks in return for a wild strawberry or raspberry. The fox often eats earthworms too, as well as bird's eggs and larger insects; in many places, it exploits human refuse, and it is notorious for helping itself from poorly secured henhouses. The carcasses of large mammals can be its salvation in the winter. The fox is versatile and adaptable, a true opportunist.

Its kinship with the dog isn't hard to see either. The tracks alone make it clear that the fox is a canine, and the long snout is another sign. Moreover, the fox's skeleton—like that of a dog—is more rigid than that of a cat. Its forepaws cannot be freely rotated. If a tame fox licks your hand, it feels soft like a dog's tongue, not rasping like the lick of a cat. If you get that close to a fox, you'll also notice that in many ways it behaves like a dog. The body languages of foxes, wolves, and dogs are "clearly part of the same 'linguistic family,'" as I read, aptly enough, in the introduction to a book about the behavior of different canine species.

FAR BACK IN TIME, the fox's family tree started out with our own. We mammals have lived on Earth for more than 200 million years, and the forebears of the carnivorans—the branch of the mammalian family tree to which foxes, dogs, and cats all belong—split away from the rest of us a good while before the catastrophe 66 million years ago that wiped out the big dinosaurs and many other types of animals, probably as a consequence of a meteorite strike. Shortly after this catastrophe, the carnivorans split into several branches. One of these led to the felids (family Felidae, cats), another to the canids (family Canidae, dogs). The latter evolved in North America and were isolated there as long as that part of the world had no overland links to the other continents.

Topsy, the red fox, and all other canids now living stem from the genus *Leptocyon*, which originated in North America some 34 million years ago. All the various *Leptocyon* species were small and long-bodied, weighing less than 4.4 pounds, and had sharp snouts with delicate teeth, probably best suited to snapping up quick-moving little animals. It is also likely that they ate other food, such as fruit. Roughly 10 million years ago, the forebears of the wolf among the small *Leptocyon* canids split away from the forebears of the red fox. Over time, the wolf's ancestors evolved massive bodies, with neck muscles, jaws, and teeth designed to grip, kill, and tear up large animals; they also acquired the endurance needed to wear out their prey, as well as the psychological traits it takes to hunt effectively in packs. The fox's predecessors, on the other hand, retained a lifestyle more like that of the *Leptocyon* animals they originated from: small prey, solitary hunting by stealth, and an eclectic diet. That said, the fox has also become much larger than its ancestors. It has evolved its own adaptations to a vulpine life as a mouse specialist and a flexible omnivore.

Nowadays, the red fox and the wolf belong to two different branches of the family Canidae (dogs). The whole of the fox's side of the family goes by the Latin name Vulpini, which consists of relatively small species. You would generally recognize them as some kind of fox. The biggest of them is the red fox, which is also both the most numerous and the most widespread. Another fox, the Arctic fox, lives in the northernmost regions of the world, including Scandinavia, northern Canada, and Alaska. In North America, other species include the kit fox, which lives in the deserts of the American Southwest, and the swift fox, which lives in the grasslands. The wolf's branch of the family, Canini, encompasses species such as the coyote in North America and the jackals found in Africa and Eurasia. The wolf is the biggest of the canids and its descendant, the dog, has achieved a larger population size than any other carnivoran through its partnership with humans. There may be as many as a billion dogs in the world. Most of them are ownerless and reproduce freely on the streets or at landfill sites and other places in the vicinity of humans—a fact that is easy to forget in the parts of the world where pretty much all dogs have a dog bowl and a name.

The red fox is often just called the fox—particularly in areas where it is the only, or most abundant, fox species. Its Latin name, *Vulpes vulpes*, means simply "fox fox." Foxy McFoxface. The fox-fox himself. It evolved into a separate species after the canids found their way out of North America a few million years ago. The red fox may have originated in the Middle East; at any rate, it ultimately spread across much of Asia and Europe, as well as North Africa, went on to conquer its forebears' continent—North America— and was introduced into Australia by humans. It can be found in almost all habitats, from highlands to coastal regions, from metropolis to wilderness, and from the deserts of Saudi Arabia to the Arctic tundra. Its appearance and size vary a great deal depending on the climate. In southern desert regions, the red foxes have pale fur and massive ears, and they weigh less than half as much as their northern siblings—yet they are also red foxes. The species can adapt to most conditions and is, in short, a huge success. No other carnivoran is so widespread, apart from the domestic dog and the house cat.

ALTHOUGH THE FOX HUNTS ALONE, it is a social animal by comparison with the cat. The fox has a family. The core consists of the adult parents, who may stay together from one year to the next if they manage to live that long. The couple shares a home range where they spend most of their time. In springtime in particular, they defend this home range, or at least parts of it, against intruders of their own species; when the area is defended in this way, it is often referred to as a territory.

The male and female fox sleep separately. In autumn and winter, they spend a lot of time roaming alone, but each spring and summer, they work together closely to bring up a litter of cubs. Although the male does not usually enter the den, the mother and young rely on the food he delivers at the entrance, from the last stage of gestation and throughout the time when the cubs are helpless and in need of their mother's warmth and milk. After the cubs start to venture out of the den, both parents bring them food. Sometime in the late summer or autumn, the young are big enough to manage by themselves and seek their fortunes outside their parents' home range. They may become sexually mature in the first year of their life, in time for the mating season in the late winter.

There are numerous variations on this basic theme. Two-timing during mating season is one—it happens among red foxes just as it does among most species that are socially monogamous. The result is that the cubs sometimes have a genetic father in addition to the one that brings them food. Even the family group that shares the home range on a daily basis may be extended. It is not uncommon for one or several adult daughters to remain in their parents' home range, helping to feed and tend their younger siblings. Now and then extra males and unrelated individuals may also join the family group. Most often, only the dominant vixen has cubs and actively prevents the others from reproducing, but the rules of vulpine life are rarely set in stone. Two or more vixens may have litters within the same home range. Sometimes, they may combine their litters and look after them together. There may be polygamy, or the pack's life may be downright promiscuous. Roughly speaking, the groups become larger and more complicated the better their access to food, and the fox's family life apparently diverges most dramatically from the simple nuclear family model in built-up areas where it is common for people to feed foxes in their gardens, a custom that is particularly established in parts of England.

The fathers' active role in raising the next generation is unusual among mammals as a whole. But these caring fathers and the flexible family groups, in which even more individuals can help take care of the litter, are typical of canids. This family model is often said to be one of the reasons for the success of the canids. In fact, family groups centered on two parents working together exist among all canids, with the exception of the one we know best. Among domestic dogs, the males have largely lost the strong caring and providing instinct we also see in male wolves. When living among people, food is apparently easy enough to come by for females to bring up their litters alone, even for dogs that live free and independent lives. The dog also differs from all other canids in its ability to reproduce more than once a year—and the lack of any synchronized mating season. Even so, our dogs have retained one clear trace of the canids' communal family system. When Topsy first came into heat, we were warned that she might experience a pseudopregnancy afterward. When that happens, the hormones rage as if the animal really were gestating a litter: her teats grow and she may display striking concern for her toys or anything else reminiscent of a puppy. Topsy apparently does not belong to the 50 percent of female dogs that experience such pseudopregnancies. But this phenomenon is, at any rate, a legacy of the canids' original family system, which the fox also follows. These physical changes, which occur in females without puppies in many canid species, probably prepare them to act as mothers to puppies born to others.

WHEN IT COMES TO THE FOX, the conclusion must be that it is a complex character. It is a catlike canine. It is a family-loving loner, which cooperates when raising its young but hunts and eats alone. It is a stealthy mouse hunter designed for high leaps, and an adaptable omnivore that seizes whatever opportunities come its way.

Now the Fox Sleeps Too

WHEN OUR SONS WERE LITTLE, we used to sing them a Norwegian lullaby. It's a sleep-inducing little tune whose brief lyrics state—quite untruly—that all the animals lie down and go to sleep at night, even the fox. It sleeps with its tail beneath its head. The mere thought of this song is still enough to make my eyelids droop.

The trouble with real foxes is that they don't actually sleep at the same time as us humans, a fact of which I was painfully aware as I cycled away from home at quarter past four in the pitch darkness of a chilly July morning in the hope of seeing a fox. My back was stiff, my thoughts sluggish, and no one else was out and about in my neighborhood; no one was driving along the country road either, apart from a bus, its empty seats lit up. On the other side of a field, I heard a dry bark that could well have been a red fox. Possibly. There was no time to investigate though, because after doing a fair amount of scouting, I'd identified a special spot farther out into the country-side where the terrain was a patchwork of woodland

and cultivated fields, a place where the chance of a fox showing itself should be especially high, and I was keen to be in place at dawn—because the fox is not exclusively nocturnal. Although it certainly favors dusk and daybreak, as well as the intervening hours of darkness, it also hunts in the daylight. In areas where it is keen to avoid being seen by humans, it tends to make the most of the early summer mornings, when the sun rises well before people do.

Close to my destination, as I was making my way through a dark stand of trees on foot, I met a badger. It had probably just finished its night shift and was heading home to its sett. At any rate, it was waddling along the way badgers do, snout to the forest floor, and it didn't notice me until it was two or three yards away. Then it lifted its black-and-white striped head, widened its small eyes, and dashed off. It didn't run far. Before it was quite out of sight, the badger turned around and started walking back, only to find that I was still standing there. It fled into the woods again, returned, then had to beat a retreat once more, seemingly surprised to discover that someone was blocking its path this time too. The fourth time the badger approached, it stopped and looked at me. Then, plucking up its courage, it ran past me as fast as its legs would carry it and continued on down the path. Perhaps force of habit conquered fear. Perhaps this was the precise route the badger took home every single morning, and perhaps it was tired of it all and couldn't face the idea of a detour or delay. At any rate, that's how I think of the badger: shortsighted, stubborn, dim.

The spot where I met the badger was right where I had been planning to head off the path and find a hiding place on the edge of the wood, facing the freshly mown meadow. Still sleepy, I unfolded my moss-green foam sit pad, unscrewed the lid of my thermos of coffee, poured myself a cup, and sat down to wait. Wagtails scurried and flew. A roe deer doe passed by, and a bit later, a buck followed on her trail, scenting the air. The sun rose. First it touched the treetops in the west, then it reached down into the meadow, while the oak trees continued to shade the place where I sat—which was fine by me. The shade provided cover. Whenever I raised binoculars or coffee cup, I tried to use slow, smooth movements to avoid drawing attention to myself. The cry of a common buzzard sounded in the forest on the other side of the meadow. Then I heard another, coming from elsewhere. When the birds came into view, they turned out not to be buzzards at all, but Eurasian jays mimicking them. One of them flew over me and sat in an oak tree directly behind me. First it repeated the buzzard's cry, *kee ya, kee ya*, then it made a kind of whimpering noise so much like a human being that I couldn't help smiling, and finally it followed up with a couple of its own hoarse shrieks. I hunkered down and hoped the fox wasn't keeping track of all this from the edge of the forest on the other side of the meadow. When at last I turned to look for the jay, it flew off.

I spied my first fox at quarter to six—a flash of color out on one of the midfield islets that prompted me to raise my binoculars. There it lay, stretched out, copper-red in the morning sun with a chalk-white breast. The fox scratched its shoulder with its hind leg, just like Topsy does. It seemed small and delicate; perhaps it was one of this year's litter. When a roe deer came out of the forest directly behind it, the fox didn't react much, but it kept turning its head abruptly as if it had heard something, and after a while it got up and vanished into the long grass of the midfield islet. I saw it again a few minutes later, out on the mown meadow, where it seemed to listen and scout for prey before disappearing into the forest over at the other side of the field and vanishing from sight.

A noisy family of green woodpeckers crossed the meadow, darting into the forest above my head. Some starlings practiced formation flying. A good half hour after I'd spotted the first fox, along came another. This one seemed bigger and darker than its predecessor and was carrying something large in its jaws. A bird. I think it was a mallard, speckled brown—so either an adult female or one of that year's ducklings. The fox seemed to be struggling to carry its prey, and it stopped several times on its way to the edge of the forest where it too vanished, leaving me sitting there in a state of bliss. At last I had found the foxes.

Of course I came back. In the days that followed, I returned to this spot on the edge of the meadow as early in the morning as I could, hoping to see more.

Blackback

OVER THE SUMMER, I saw the dark fox I'd first spotted with a duck in its mouth many more times. She turned out to be a vixen. Her face was relatively narrow—that can be a sign—and in the photos I eventually took of her there was no sign of the pale fur between the legs that is the hallmark of a male fox seen from the rear. She also squatted down to urinate rather than cocking a hind leg. I nicknamed her Blackback, for the blackish patch of fur on her red-brown flanks, which looked something like a riding saddle and whose pattern reminded me of the African canid known as the blackbacked jackal. Her tail was pretty thin, with just a few sparse tufts of longish hair here and there. That's the kind of look that might make people suspect that a fox has mange—a disfiguring and often fatal disease—but I don't really think there was anything wrong with Blackback. She seemed otherwise healthy and energetic. There was no sign of the bald patches that are the clear hallmark of a mangy fox. Most likely, she was mother to a lively litter of cubs, and her summer coat was simply worn out from her exertions through the spring and early summer.

The very next time I sat on the edge of the forest, I saw Blackback with a smaller flame-red fox, which I assumed to be a cub—maybe the same one I'd seen the day before. They lay together, resting. Now and then they would put their heads together, so their snouts touched. Later, they got up on their hind legs and had a wrestling match, in which the little fox was allowed to topple the bigger fox. Immediately afterward, they vanished out of sight. In the days that followed, I generally saw only one fox at a time, although I did sometimes catch sight of two heads or two pairs of ears poking up out of the long grass. Sometimes I would hear hissing and whines that may have been the sound of fox cubs fighting. A grown male fox made an appearance in the area—I dubbed him Choccy for the somewhat chocolaty tone of his fur—and I assumed he was Blackback's partner, although I never saw the two animals together. The foxes I was watching out on the meadow were probably a family with large cubs, which had left the den and established a base out on the midfield islets, where the parents would bring the cubs food while they practiced catching their own.

Blackback—she was the one I saw most often—proved to be a skilled hunter. She would comb the landscape, especially along the edges of the midfield islets and the stream that crossed the meadow just a stone's throw below the spot where I sat, and find something edible at regular intervals. She didn't turn up with any more birds, but on several occasions, I heard panicky mallards down in the lake and guessed that, schooled by bitter experience, they were warning each other about the fox. Even the songbirds frequently sounded the alarm. Now and then you could tell from the way their jarring cries and tweets moved from place to place that danger was approaching, and sometimes my suspicions would be confirmed by the appearance of a fox coming from precisely the area where the birds had raised the alarm. Otherwise, the fox could show up anywhere—in the distance as a dark patch, or so close that I had to hold my breath to avoid discovery. When the north wind blew, I avoided my regular spot, so that my scent wouldn't be blown out onto the meadow, betraying my presence; apart from that one time when the click of my camera made the fox stare hard in my direction, I don't think the foxes in the meadow to the south of me had a clue that I was sitting there on the edge of the forest. If you sit still, you're hard to see.

One moonlit morning hour when I was walking along the farm road, I spotted Blackback's dark silhouette in the nighttime mist that crept low across the meadow closest to the farm buildings. She sat there looking at me. Only sometime after I'd stopped and lifted my binoculars to my eyes did she get up and slink away among the trees. I can't have scared her all that much because just twenty minutes after I'd sat down in my usual spot, she came into view again, attention focused on one of midfield islets. Soon she stopped, body tense. She leaped high into the air and vanished into the long grass. When she backed out again, tail first, she had a mouse-sized object in her jaws. She dropped what I assumed to be a field vole onto the mown grass, then started to stalk it, attacked it, picked it up again, and dropped it. Several times, she leaped into the air, pouncing once again upon the prey she had allowed to escape. There was no doubt about it— she was playing with this little rodent, roughly the way cats do. After a while, the field vole appeared to give up all attempts at escape, either because it had passed out or was simply paralyzed with fear, or perhaps because its tiny heart had already stopped beating; at any rate, Blackback started to pick it up and toss her head so that the vole's body flew through the air in an arc and landed a couple of the vixen's body lengths away in the grass—then she sprinted after it to capture the runaway. She did this time and time again; in all, I saw her hurl her prey away ten times before she eventually lay down and—so it seemed—swallowed it in a single mouthful. I had seen this type of play before too. Topsy enjoyed throwing and catching the sweet cherries she found on the ground beneath our tree, and when she got bored indoors, she would sometimes mess around with a bit of dry food from her bowl in the same way. What I found surprising was that the vixen could spend time and energy on play, as I'd assumed this was a luxury reserved for cubs who were still being fed by their parents—and pets, of course. Perhaps Blackback was in a playful mood just then because she was busy training her cubs to hunt for themselves, but there were no cubs to be seen this morning. I chose to think that she simply had enough spare energy to indulge in some fun—a bit like me, who had nothing better to do than sit there on the forest's edge staring and speculating.

It's not hard to imagine the pleasure of a fox well fed enough after the night's hunt to take a break and play with her prey as the morning sun starts to spread its heat. This same capacity for empathy also makes us shudder at the thought of being pursued by a cheery monster a thousand times heavier than us who's decided to entertain herself by granting us one last chance to flee before the kill. We can identify just as easily with the fox as with the field vole because neither are entirely alien beings. They, like us, have drunk milk and felt the warmth of a mother's body. They, like us, played their way into skills early on in life. In fact, if we're to believe the very latest studies of the mammalian family tree, the field vole is a closer relative of humans than the fox is; yet I'm convinced that the fox is closer to us in mentality and way of life. In size alone, we operate on a more similar scale. If you happen across a white fox skull on the forest floor, the set of teeth you'll see is far more recognizable than the teeth in the cranium of a field vole or a roe deer, because the fox isn't just a mouse snatcher; it is also an all-around omnivore, like us.

Blackback got up again and stared into the long grass. Eventually, she repeated the fox's distinctive mouse pounce—jumping high in the air, paws outstretched—but this time, she returned with empty jaws. She gave herself a little shake, as if she were embarrassed but trying to look unruffled in case anyone was watching. That resembled behavior I've seen from dogs, cats, and wild birds of prey—people too, for that matter—after a failed maneuver. Many kinds of animals need to preserve their dignity—a lack of regard in the eyes of others can be dangerous.

Halfway between the rocky outcrops of two of the midfield islets, Blackback sat down, face turned in my direction. She didn't seem to have seen me this time, but I sat quiet as a mouse. Shortly afterward, she caught some prey out on the open meadow. The silhouette that dangled from her jaws was long and slack, perhaps a frog; if so, this latest victim was a cold body that had never known either love or the lack of it, because enduring relationships and the nurturing of offspring do not form part of the frog's existence. The lifeworld of amphibians is infinitely more difficult for us to empathize with than those of mammals. Our evolutionary histories are separated by a deeper gulf of time, more than 300 million years, and our ways of life are so different. Blackback swallowed down her prey without any great fanfare.

The fox vanished out of sight, and the sounds of a summer morning started to emerge. The reigning roe deer buck bellowed close by in the forest. Wood pigeons cooed on all sides and for a while, the rarer stock dove was audible too. Planes and cars rumbled, if you tuned into that frequency. At seven o'clock, just when I was getting ready to pack up, I unexpectedly caught sight of Blackback again, and this time she had caught a larger prey. The animal hung brown and lifeless from her jaws for the brief instant it was visible. A European water vole, apparently—a larger relative of the field voles. Blackback didn't play this time. She stood with her rump in the air working on her prey, either eating it up or burying it for later, the way foxes do when their bellies are full.

Of Mice and Voles

ONE OF THE REASONS why red foxes have become so numerous and widespread is that they are omnivores that help themselves to whatever is at hand. Another reason the species has done so well is that it has a particular talent for catching rodents, which are the most numerous and successful group of mammals. The close to 2,500 rodent species known to us worldwide account for more than a third of all mammal species.

Rodents form a pretty varied group, which encompasses, for example, squirrels that leap among the treetops and beavers that fell trees and build dams. That said, rodents are typically rather small animals with thin tails, such as mice and rats. Those two names don't really correspond to the scientific classification of rodents, but tend to be applied to smaller and somewhat larger species, respectively. The fox will take any kind of smaller rodent whenever the opportunity arises, but its most typical prey is a group called voles. They have shorter tails than the house mice and brown rats that people living in urban settings tend to be familiar with. Voles are also rounder in build, often have shorter ears, and move primarily by walking rather than jumping.

Small rodents of all kinds are surrounded by enemies. They include cats, foxes, snakes, and many birds of prey, including common buzzards, common kestrels, and several kinds of owls. Naturally then, mice and voles are highly alert. At the slightest sign of danger, they dash off to seek cover in a hole, a crack, or some other place where the enemy cannot reach them—and rodents living in open landscapes, like the field vole and the water vole, are especially likely to hide in tunnels and holes they have dug themselves. Familiarity with the terrain is vital. Voles, mice, and rats always need to know the way to their nearest hiding place, which might explain why they perform so well in laboratory experiments where they have to find their way through mazes. If escape seems hopeless, a small rodent may opt for an alternative: sitting still (quiet as a mouse, as the saying goes) to avoid detection. For the would-be mouse eater, it is crucial to approach unseen, and above all unheard, to ensure that its prey never has a chance to reach safety. That is why owls can fly noiselessly. That is why foxes make those long lunges.

The way foxes hunt, eat, and prepare their food is described in great detail in a little book by Canadian biologist J. David Henry called *Red Fox: The Catlike Canine*. Henry spent years observing red foxes in Prince Albert National Park in Saskatchewan, a part of western Canada. The foxes in the national park had not been hunted or trapped for half a century, so they weren't especially scared of people. With the aid of patience and treats, Henry was eventually allowed to follow the foxes on their daily rounds of hunting.

The foxes liked to follow paths, animal tracks, and roadside verges. Henry thought it was easier for them to move soundlessly along well-trodden routes like these because there were fewer twigs or other loose material on the ground that would make a noise. If the fox heard potential prey in the vegetation, such as a mouse or a chipmunk, it would stop, turn to the side, and stretch its neck as it stared attentively toward the place where it had heard something. A fox with its head lifted in this way is almost always on the hunt, Henry writes. Perhaps the fox would scent the air or perhaps it would tilt its head, first to one side then to the other, to home in on the precise location of the sound. Sometimes, the fox chose to sneak closer. Then it lowered its body and head and took slow, tentative steps, possibly lifting its paw up again to find a better place to set it down. Foxes do not just have whiskers on their noses, like cats, but also have similar vibrissae (special sensory hairs) on their legs. Once the fox was near enough, it would raise its head into hunting position again. As soon as it had located the prey, it would crouch down, then pounce on its victim and try to pin it firmly to the ground. If the attack was successful, it might either kill the prey at once, with several bites, or perhaps take it off to some suitable place to play with it "like a cat with a mouse," Henry writes.

He went on to note that the fox took a quite different approach to hunting birds and tree-climbing squirrels—in other words, animals that fled upward when they spied the fox and primarily relied on vision to detect potential dangers. The fox's method for hunting these animals was to creep closer—body as low to the ground as possible, even if that meant making the odd noise—launch into a quick sprint and, finally, lunge forward to trap the prey in its teeth. This kind of attack usually failed. The fox used a similar strategy with hares and rabbits, first creeping closer, body low, and then engaging in a frantic pursuit as soon as the prey sensed danger. As for insects, the fox would catch them whenever the opportunity arose. Neither the effort nor the reward were all that great, but the fox generally succeeded because grasshoppers and the like were so unsophisticated in their escape attempts.

The fox ate up its prey as soon as it had captured it, Henry observed, until it was full. Around a pound of meat tended to be enough. That's equivalent to perhaps ten fully grown mice. Once its hunger was sated, it started squirreling away food by burying supplies, which served as the fox's insurance in case of injury, worsening weather conditions, or a failure to find enough food for one reason or another. Many animals, including corvids and other red foxes, would loot these stores if they could, so it was important to hide the food well. Every morsel was buried separately and distributed over large areas. First the fox would dig a little hole, perhaps four inches deep, and deposit the food in it. Then it would shovel the earth back into place, packing it firmly into the hole with its snout. Finally, it would camouflage the food store by arranging leaves and debris so that the ground looked undisturbed. During the winter, Henry observed a fox burying the valuable hind parts of a hare. Not only did it carefully smooth over the upper layer of snow with its snout to erase all signs of activity—it also erased every single footprint as it backed away from the secret spot.

MY OWN FOX-WATCHING happened at a greater distance than Henry's and was more sporadic than his months-long stays in the wilderness. Even so, the fox drew me out into nature and into the landscape too. As I scouted for the beautiful predator with its red fur and white-tipped tail, I found I was developing an unexpected interest in the tiny, timid mammals that abounded in the terrain. The very smallest of them, known as shrews, rustled frantically around me in the grass and withered foliage as I sat still and waited, emitting squeaks so high that they were on the very edge of my hearing range. Shrews are not rodents and are a rather different shape from ordinary mice, if you see them close-up. That opportunity most often presents itself when you stumble across a dead shrew in the middle of a track after a fox, cat, or bird has killed it, only to find that this prey tastes downright disgusting. Despite the unappetizing flavor, a fox will eat shrews now and then; I suppose it depends on how hungry it is.

One time when I was sitting there on the look-out for foxes, a field vole peeped out from among the stems and stalks and looked at me with perfectly round black eyes set beneath ears half-buried in its fur. When it turned away, I saw its remarkably short tail. Out on the meadows and on the edge of the forest, I found holes and tunnels that the field voles had dug, as well as the tennis-ball-sized entrances to the den of the larger water vole. When I set up a wildlife camera down by the water vole holes in a drainage ditch—the kind of camera that starts filming if anything moves—I got to see the water vole; it was a bit like an enormous field vole and a bit like a miniature beaver. The water vole dug and dug. It sat on the platform of earth outside its hole nibbling away on grass and other plants, and when a rain shower filled the bed of the ditch, it was as likely to swim as to walk. The close-up shots from my wildlife camera also gave me my first sighting of what was almost certainly a bank vole, which prefers the forest, where it lives up to its Norwegian name of *klatremus*—climbing mouse—by clambering around in trees. It revealed which species it was by its tail, which was short but still longer than the field vole's; it also had reddish fur high up on its back.

We miss out on a lot by always lifting our gaze. If it wasn't for the fox, I probably would have continued to overlook these small animals, but each of them has its own particular appearance and lifestyle; they eat and are eaten, they sleep, live, mate, care for their young, play, compete, and fight. And while each individual vole or mouse may be small, there are so many of them that they are crucially important for larger animals too. They can even sate a hungry fox.

Why Roe Deer Fear the Fox

THE BARKS THAT RANG across the meadow sounded like a kind of abrupt burping. The noise came from a doe that was dashing toward the edge of the forest, and neither her high leaps nor her warning barks left any room for doubt—she had detected danger. Shortly afterward, Blackback came trotting along from the same direction. It seemed likely that she was the threat that had caused the alarm—and at roughly the spot where the roe deer had vanished among the trees, the vixen sat down and stared into the forest. Next to show up was the buck. He had probably heard the doe's warning. At any rate, he stopped, looked over at Blackback, and urinated a bit before walking calmly but firmly toward the vixen, until she got up and made herself scarce.

THE FOX RARELY POSES a threat to an adult roe deer. However, it is a mortal danger to the white-spotted fawns. When scientists doing fieldwork in an area roughly an hour's drive from my home tagged newborn fawns with radio transmitters, they found that one in five were killed by foxes during the summer—and were often dragged home to the cubs. Some of the carcasses and radio collars were found in foxes' dens. Research conducted in various parts of Scandinavia indicates that the fox is the leading cause of death among young fawns. (It might surprise some North American readers to learn that red foxes are predators of deer fawns, given their relative size. But the roe deer is considerably smaller than most North American deer, while European red foxes are often larger than their North American counterparts—and have a similar predatory relationship to deer fawns as coyotes in North America.)

As long as the mother of a threatened fawn is there, she can usually see off a persistent fox; but during the early weeks of their lives, fawns spend a lot of time alone. They lie hidden on the ground, waiting for their mother to come and suckle them. The fox is an expert tracker of the fawns, and it seems that one of its methods is to search the terrain around a doe with udders full of milk. The does face a dilemma: The best grazing is usually exactly where the foxes are. And during the summer, the does need nourishing food to produce milk for one, two, or even three fawns. What's more, roe deer are picky herbivores that prefer juicy leaves, buds, and stalks containing plenty of sugar and not much fiber. The meadow that I watched from my regular spot on the edge of the forest was used to grow animal feed, but the grass crops were probably not the main attraction for the roe deer. They gravitated toward the forest edge, where the meadow flowered, as well as similar flowering areas on the midfield islets, along the drainage ditches, and in areas of old meadow that were lying fallow or had been set aside for grazing livestock. These kinds of species-rich meadows, where all sorts of plants have a chance to compete for space, are among the very best grazing spots for roe deer. The terrain is tempting but dangerous; it is also a paradise for rodents—and therefore foxes. This is why fawns that hide in the meadow to be close to their mothers are so vulnerable to predation by foxes.

There were plenty of signs that the deer and foxes were getting on each other's nerves during those summer mornings in the meadow. I saw a buck lower his antlers and charge at a fox, which leaped aside. I saw a fox stalking a doe and fawn from a fair distance. Once I saw an unaccompanied fawn cross the meadow and hide in the lush vegetation along the drainage ditch; an hour later, after the fawn was reunited with its mother, I noticed that both of them were standing there, noses up, sniffing the air. Suddenly the male fox, Choccy, emerged from the nearby ditch. He was dripping wet. He must have approached under cover of the dense foliage before appearing in almost exactly the same spot where the fawn had previously hidden, and now he took up a position just three or four yards away from the roe deer. The atmosphere was tense. None of them made a move.

MUCH OF THE DRAMA in a roe deer's life is compressed into the bright weeks of summer—birth, nurturing, rivalry, and mating. While the does wander around with swollen bellies, the bucks are busy establishing and defending their territory. Their bellows echo across forest and meadow from spring onward, and dark patches appear on the ground where the buck has scraped up the soil and scented the area to mark it as his territory. Mating takes place in late summer, while the fawns are still with their mothers. To watch roebucks swaggering about or chasing each other across the meadow on a summer morning feels like witnessing a scene from the dawn of time. But while it is true that these are ancient behavioral patterns, roe deer are newcomers to these parts; not until the last century did they become a common sight in Norway. During the millennia since Northern Europe emerged from the last Ice Age, the species has probably been absent from most of the Scandinavian Peninsula, and mainly in evidence in southern Sweden.

Unlike the roe deer, the fox has lived up here in the north almost as long as humans. But its population too has increased. During the postwar years, many more foxes were shot in Norway than previously, and these hunting statistics almost certainly indicate that foxes became more numerous. There are many explanations for this, but an abundance of roe deer and other cervids is one of them. The fawns are not of primary importance. In summer, a wide variety of food is available, so foxes that specialize in tracking down fawns for a few weeks could also get enough food by hunting other prey. More importantly, meat from roe deer and other cervids saves many foxes from starving during the winter when mice and voles are scarce. Every autumn, tens of thousands of deer and moose are shot. When hunters abandon their slaughter waste in forests and fields, that gives the fox a chance to store up supplies for the winter. Over the winter months, carcasses of cervids that die from starvation, disease, traffic collisions, or other causes are an important food source, and if the snow is deep enough the fox can even kill an adult roe deer itself. I once saw a recording from a wildlife camera in a snowy part of Norway that showed a roe deer running for its life along a forest trail on a winter night, with a fox in hot pursuit.

Toward Fall

AS THE DAYS started to grow noticeably shorter, there were also fewer foxes to be seen from my regular spot on the edge of the forest. The cubs were grown now. They roamed over a larger area. One morning as I came cycling along, I spotted a lone fox out on the meadow at the very second that it also noticed me. From a distance, it looked like the adult animals, but its helpless behavior betrayed it as a young fox, born in the spring. It hunkered down and tried to spy on me through the grass. Although I remained standing there, binoculars raised and bicycle leaning against my hip, it soon resumed its attempts at mouse catching. You could tell from its lunges that it was unlikely to catch a thing.

In late summer, it's urgent for the young foxes to learn to catch their own food. The parents scale back their feeding and, in the transition period, the young animals probably rely mostly on earthworms and other simple prey to keep body and soul together. As autumn advances, they are faced with a major decision: whether to remain in their parents' home range or try their luck in the big, wide world. If they stay, they must resign themselves to a life of subservience. As a rule, the younger members of a family group are lower-ranking and must constantly display submissiveness if they want to avoid a beating. The fox's behavioral repertoire in this respect is familiar to us dog owners—a submissive individual crawls, lowers its head, lays its ears back, wags its tail, and whines, and may also lie on its back. If two foxes of differing rank know each other well and are not engaged in any particular conflict, fear doesn't necessarily come into the picture. In a fox couple that shares the home range, the vixen is ordinarily subordinate to the male. Other adult members of the family group are subordinate to the dominant pair and have their own separate rankings among themselves.

Topsy and I developed our own greeting ritual—which is a bit like that of the foxes—after I started to show her that she mustn't jump on me in excitement by simply turning my back on her every time she did so. Now, instead, she presses herself to the ground, wagging her tail with all her might, and when I stretch out a hand to her, she often turns over onto her back so that I can scratch her belly. She is very keen to lick my hand, even though she knows that I generally protest. If allowed, she would lick my face too. The mood can be just as friendly when two foxes meet, but if a subordinate member of the family group challenges the prevailing order, or if a high-ranking fox tries to drive a member out of the group, battles can break out and things can get heated.

If any cubs do remain with the parents, they tend to be vixens. The male cubs generally leave the parents' home range over the course of the fall. Those that leave go looking for an unoccupied home range and a partner, but success is far from certain. Mortality rates among young foxes are high. What's more, many of those that do survive their first winter—mostly males—end up living an itinerant life. The resulting reserve of homeless animals, combined with the fox's capacity for lengthy migrations, means that any home range that becomes free is quickly occupied again. Swedish and Norwegian researchers who tagged red foxes with GPS transmitters some years back were surprised to find just how far some foxes roamed. For example, one young Swedish male, whom the researchers dubbed Stefansson, traveled 180 miles as the crow flies in just twenty-two days. This is even more impressive once you take into account all the detours and backtracking. A young vixen called Gunnel covered more than 600 miles. Admittedly, the journey took her a hundred days, but much of that time was spent on three lengthy stops along the way. Perhaps she was trying out possible homes or getting to know potential partners before deciding whether to stay or travel onward.

For settled foxes, the home range may extend over several dozen square miles in barren environments, such as up in the mountains or in the North. In such cases, it is, of course, difficult for the fox to patrol the boundaries of its territory assiduously from day to day. In my neck of the woods, by the Oslo Fjord, the home ranges are likely limited to a few square miles— because the more fertile the landscape, and the more it is characterized by agriculture and human settlement, the closer together the foxes will live. In areas where the home ranges are small and rich in resources, foxes are also more diligent about policing their boundaries. These often follow roads, field borders, and the like and may move as a result of constant boundary disputes and conflicts. Foxes mark their boundaries with scent—including urine and excrement—and chase off potential intruders. In British suburbs, where many people feed foxes in their gardens, home ranges as small as ten acres have been recorded. That is equivalent to a square whose sides are roughly 660 feet long. Even so, almost the entirety of a fox's life can play out within an area as small as this. Generally speaking, territory is most fiercely defended during the breeding season in the spring and summer, when the resources in the home range are needed to feed the litter. Over the autumn, the patrolling is less thorough.

In September, I abandoned my morning trips to observe foxes out on the meadow. Although the hours

I'd spent watching laid-back foxes get on with their daily lives had left me keen for more, too many of my latest excursions had been fruitless. Until spring, I thought. Then I would track down a fox's den and try to follow the family right from the start. In the meantime, I sat indoors as the fall rain pelted the walls, absorbed in books and articles about foxes, and I speculated whether the ones I'd watched this summer would survive the hunting season.

Foxhunt

FALL IS HUNTING SEASON in Norway. But for red foxes, the season is unusually long—it opens as early as July 15 and lasts all the way up until April 15 of the following year. The point of the three-month closed season is to prevent small cubs from being orphaned and thereby doomed to starvation—but hunting starts again before the young have left their parents' home range, so it's open season on the species throughout most of the year as long as the landowner allows hunting. It's hardly surprising, then, that foxes in rural Norway are timid. There, as in the countryside elsewhere in Europe, the life of a fox that places its trust in humans is most likely to end with a bullet from a rifle or a body full of shot.

WHY SHOOT FOXES? The carcass has hardly any economic value. Back in the Stone Age, people probably ate fox meat, but it's been a long time since that was popular fare; it is already close to five hundred years since Olaus Magnus of Sweden had this to say about Scandinavians' exploitation of game: "It is only the meat of foxes and wolves that men reject, since these beasts are unclean by nature and prone to various diseases, especially rabies." That said, the fox's thick winter pelt has always been prized by those living in colder climes. Back in the sixteenth century, people would sew clothes and bedding from fox furs, and since fox fur blankets were light and retained heat well, they were especially suitable for old people— according to Magnus, himself in his sixties. He claimed to be the Archbishop of Sweden, although he was living in exile when he wrote his great work, *A Description of the Northern Peoples*, in the papal city of Rome, because Magnus was still Catholic, whereas the Nordic countries had adopted the Protestant teachings of Martin Luther. Perhaps the bishop's toes froze in those magnificent Italian stone buildings during the winter. Perhaps he missed having a Nordic fox fur blanket. At any rate, he had a great deal to say about foxes, hunting, and furs.

Red foxes are everywhere, Magnus wrote of the Far North. "They prove an easy prey for crafty hunters and swift dogs, who follow their tracks through the snow." The somewhat credulous bishop also claimed that foxes would ride on the backs of goats to escape from hunters. A more believable piece of information he relayed was that some fox furs were far more valuable than those of the ordinary red fox—furs in other, rare colors, especially black fox furs. He had the impression that the Russians obtained these black pelts somewhere far to the east, and he also suspected that they were sometimes fabricated by dyeing ordinary red fox furs. In reality, these precious black fox furs may have come by ship from North America, where European explorers and traders had just begun to gain a foothold. In North America, many wild red foxes have black fur. The tips of the hair may often be silver-gray too—hence the term "silver foxes." The hunt for rare and beautiful types of fur from many different species would become an important stimulus for the European conquest of the cold regions of the globe, such as Siberia, Alaska, and Canada. Through much of the past century, fox furs were still worth hunting for, in Norway as elsewhere, and even today, you'll hear young foxhunters talk about the "fur trapper's life" as an inspiring legend. The reality is that it's almost impossible to sell wild fox pelts any longer. The hunters are outcompeted by fur farmers, who produce furs that are thicker, longer, and glossier.

One factor that *is* an important driver of foxhunting these days is excitement. The fox's intelligence and alertness make it a worthy opponent in hunters' eyes; getting within firing distance of a fox is described as a genuine challenge. What's more—according to those who write about hunting in books, magazines, and informational materials for hunting associations—the foxhunting tradition is a valuable cultural heritage that should be conserved. As far as hunters are concerned, the fox competes with them for game, and they consider foxhunting to be a socially useful activity, since it ensures that more roe deer, hares, or game fowl will be available to hunt. The competition between fox and hunter is real enough. Research shows that where there are fewer foxes, other small game is more abundant. The question is whether hunting actually does anything to reduce fox populations, because foxes reproduce rapidly and can migrate long distances, so free home ranges are quickly occupied again—at least in areas where living conditions are good and fox populations relatively dense. That means it would be hard for hobby hunters to succeed in regulating the number of foxes. One hunting magazine article cited an unnamed zoologist, who speculated that hunters' efforts to outsmart foxes by laying out bait for them might actually serve more as a supplementary food source for foxes during the winter than an effective means of population control. That may be a fair point. Hunting literature generally advises leaving food at the bait station over a period of time, so that the fox gets into the habit of stopping by. In one foxhunting publication produced by the Norwegian Association of Hunters and Anglers, the following advice is offered to hunters wanting to catch foxes in live traps—where the animals end up shut into a kind of crate:

> It will be very useful to start leaving food there long before the trapping takes place, preferably months in advance. That makes the trap a pleasant place for the fox, with plenty of good food. It

is extremely important for there to be food in the trap at all times!

Traps have been used for foxhunting in Scandinavia from ancient times; Bishop Olaus Magnus talks about how foxes that catch a foot in a trap sometimes bite off their own leg to get free. Luckily, steel-jaw leghold traps, which place animals in this kind of ghastly situation, have been banned in Norway—although they are still in use across much of North America. Nowadays, the only traps permissible in Norway are those that catch the fox alive, shutting it into a cage or crate—and the traps must be checked every day. The animal is put down with a bullet.

SOME FOXHUNTERS simply track the fox by following its pawprints in the snow, but of course it's quite a challenge to get within shooting distance of a sharp-eared animal using this method. That's why many hunters opt to lure the fox to them instead. One way to do this is with sound—enticing the fox with imitations of the noises made by its prey, like the cries of a young hare in distress, or the warning calls of a bird. You can buy special decoy whistles that apparently have a fair chance of persuading the fox to leave its resting place during daylight hours to come and see what's going on. Foxhunters favor this method because it means they don't have to hunt by night. Nonetheless, baiting is probably the most common hunting method in

Norway. Foxhunters simply leave out an animal carcass, portions of dog food dipped in cod liver oil, or other foul-smelling treats, then conceal themselves and wait through the night, rifle at the ready. Some hunters use floodlights so that they can see the fox better. The hunter's hiding place may be in a barn or an outbuilding with a suitable peephole in the wall, or even inside a darkened bedroom.

IF YOU MENTION foxhunting, many people will think of Englishmen in red hunting jackets galloping headlong after a pack of hounds while the master of the hunt blows on a horn. Norway has no tradition of hunting with horse and hounds, although Denmark has a long history of it among royalty and aristocrats, as well as a newer custom called Hubertus hunting, where uniformed riders pursue the symbolic "fox," which is simply one of the other participants with a fox's tail attached to their clothing.

Hounds are used for foxhunting in Scandinavia too, but without the horses and general commotion. The "swift dogs" of the crafty hunter that Magnus referred to must have performed roughly the same task then as the dogs we call scent hounds now, which pick up the trail of a fox or hare and set off in pursuit while giving tongue—baying—so that the hunter knows where they are. The owners generally train their hounds to track a particular kind of game. You must apparently decide while a dog is still a puppy whether you want it to be a hare hound or a foxhound, and the process of choosing and training hunting hounds is a minor science in its own right, complete with its own strange, specialist vocabulary. The job of the classic scent hound, which must be a good tracker and make plenty of noise, is to give its owner a chance to shoot the fox in flight, so it is important for the hound to warn the prey of its approach; this prompts the fox to leap up from its resting place to get a head start—and makes it feel safe enough not to seek refuge in a den.

There is also another way of using scent hounds: to take the fox by surprise and scare it so much that it seeks safety in a hiding place beneath the earth. After that, the hound must stand there giving tongue to alert the hunters to the prey's whereabouts.

And what do the hunters do after the fox has gone to earth? That's right, they deploy yet another dog. A den dog. It may be a terrier or a dachshund, but the main thing is that it must be small and brave (some might say rash) enough to creep down the dark tunnels and confront a desperate foe. As I mentioned earlier, training dogs for the hunt requires highly specialized knowledge. There are also two types of den dogs. One has the task of chasing the fox into a dead end and blocking its exit by lying down and barking with all its might, so that the fox is too scared to try to get past it. If the fox tries to break out, the dog must "defend itself," as the hunting literature somewhat euphemistically puts it. Dachshunds are often used for this purpose. Once the fox is trapped down in the den, the hunter's work begins. "Now it's time to get out spade and crowbar." The purpose of the other type of den dog is simply to chase the fox out of the den. Terriers are often the dogs for that job, and the hunting literature is full of warnings about the risk of shooting the dog instead of the prey in all the commotion when the fox suddenly decides to dash out of its den again. The placement of fellow hunters and shooting trajectories must also be planned carefully to avoid the risk of shooting each other.

Until recently, Norwegian den dogs were trained and tested using foxes that hunting clubs kept in captivity for this sole purpose. The name of the last dog-training fox in my district was Ingrid. She and her colleagues elsewhere in the country were bought from fur farmers and used in artificial dens—labyrinth-like constructions at one end of which a fox was kept in a cage. The aim was for the dog to find its way to the cage through pipe tunnels to prove that it was capable of dealing with a live fox. The dog and fox were always separated by the walls of a cage. Nonetheless, the Norwegian agency responsible for animal welfare was concerned that these foxes were being subjected to unreasonably high levels of stress. In 2020, amid protests from those in hunting circles, the use of live foxes in dog training was banned.

IF TOPSY HAD HER WAY, we would probably go hunting. She loves following trails, and she even understands what's going on if I crouch down and begin to creep forward—for example, when we are approaching a lake where I know beavers live or a den where there's a chance of seeing a fox or badger. When that happens, she goes quiet too. In fact, she can hold out for a fairly long time if I sit down and stay still so that I can watch without myself being seen; I'd estimate she keeps quiet for as long as a fairly big child. But then she gets impatient. She wonders when we're going to attack, and eventually she starts to whine, dig up the soil, or mess about with a stick. That's why she rarely comes along when the aim of a trip is to see foxes.

And there won't be any hunting expeditions for Topsy either. My way of approaching her red relatives is, and always will be, fox-watching. It's not that I advocate a general ban on shooting red foxes—more that I find it and other wild species interesting in so many ways other than as quarry. And in a world where there are fewer and fewer wild animals for every human being, I think the art most of us should be cultivating is a capacity to admire them, without necessarily wanting to hunt, shoot, catch, tame, or encroach upon them.

Twentieth Century Foxes

THERE'S SOMETHING ABOUT the fox that fires people's imaginations. In the Chinese, Japanese, and Korean traditions, there are foxes that change into humans, often beautiful women who seduce men and cause all kinds of misery. There are also fox-spirits capable of possessing people, either on their own initiative or prompted by malevolent individuals. In Europe, the wolf is better known for such shape-shifting, while the red fox appears in cheerier contexts, such as fairy tales, fables, and satires, in which animals talk and resemble humans. The fox's gender depends a bit on which of the European languages is involved. The Russian fairy-tale fox, for example, is often female and is called Elizaveta—Elizabeth—which is simply a play on words: *lisá* is the Russian word for fox. In Western Europe, however, the fox is male, with names like Reineke and Reynard, while in the Nordic countries, he's known as Mikkel Rev—Mikkel Fox. From the twentieth century onward, these fictional foxes began to feature especially frequently in children's stories—not just across Europe, but also in North America and beyond.

As a small boy, I had two music cassettes, one of which was a classic Norwegian children's musical about the animals of the Huckybucky forest. The plot largely revolved around Mikkel Rev, who had a nasty habit of eating the mice in the forest.

The musical was first written for the radio in 1953 and was later reworked as a book, a stage play, and an audiobook. Over time, it became a rich source of shared references for generations of Norwegians. The songs are such a profoundly familiar part of my childhood that I can still sing along with every word.

In the story, written by Thorbjørn Egner, the mice form an alliance with Father Bear, and together the mice-bear coalition push through a total ban on animals eating each other. The law is passed unanimously at a general assembly of the animals of the forest. Even Mikkel, the fox, feels obliged to put up his paw and vote in favor. But afterward, he finds it difficult to adapt to life as a vegetarian—until he discovers a loophole in the law and steals a whole cured ham from the storehouse of a nearby farm. That exposes the forest to a new danger: foxhunting farmers. When the hunters find Father Bear's infant cub, whom they capture and decide to try to sell to a circus, Mikkel and the mice collaborate on a rescue plan. The story ends with fellowship among all the animals of the forest and a joint celebration of Father Bear's birthday.

There was one odd thing about Egner's fox: he was stupid. *He* was the one who fell for other people's tricks, even though other stories often told us that foxes were sly—as in the Norwegian folktales collected by Asbjørnsen and Moe in the nineteenth century. In those, we learned that the bear had a short tail because Mikkel Rev once tricked him into trying ice fishing with his tail while the lake was freezing over, and that the fox gained the white tip on his tail after he took a job as a shepherd, gobbled up the entire flock he was supposed to be looking after, drank the cream at the farm, and—after the furious farmer's wife discovered how he had fooled her—had the very last white drop of cream hurled after him.

The most likely reason why the fox is such a fool in the tale of the Huckybucky forest is that the character was invented in an era when edification was of the essence, and all children's stories were expected to have a crystal-clear moral. Villains weren't supposed to have any impressive features that might encourage children to imitate them. The one mitigating trait that Egner gave the fox was that, with a little effort, he could be reformed—and more or less become a decent citizen. In this respect, the story reflected the postwar conviction that both society and the people who lived in it could change for the better.

Still, one does wonder whether an ironic smile played on the author's lips when he chose to use a decree mandating friendship between mouse and fox as the image of the social democratic, Scandinavian societal order. "Don't you think carrots are awful?" Mikkel Rev asked the children listening to the play. "What? You think carrots are nice? Well, then—you're definitely not foxes!"

Quite so. We are what we are.

When the Fox Preaches

THE FOX'S BAD REPUTATION has deep roots. The philosopher Aristotle described the fox as a sneak, who
basely hid beneath the ground and avoided scrutiny.
"That fox," said Jesus of his enemy King Herod, who
wanted to kill him. In the early Christian work *Physiologus*, the fox was directly associated with the devil.
These ideas came to color the tales told about the fox
across Europe.

But there was also another vulpine literary figure,
strongly represented in Aesop's fables—a collection
of short animal tales that were first written down in
Greek in the centuries before the Common Era, and
which later lived on as a standard component of Latin
teaching in schools. Here, the fox displays a form of
cunning intended both to amuse and impress. A good
example is the time he gets the better of his archen-
emy, the wolf, by telling the sick lion king that the
cure for his ailments is to wrap himself in a fresh
wolfskin. The short and pithy moral that follows each
fable generally encourages readers to do as the fox did.
In other words, this animal is presented at one and
the same time as a likable underdog and a dangerous

fiend—hero and villain in the same body. Such ambiguity is precisely what makes for an irresistible literary character, and in the Middle Ages, the European fox fables grew into long-form tales, long enough to fill books, just as the literary foxes were also making their appearance in church art.

Katharinenkirche, in the Hanseatic city of Lübeck in northern Germany, is among the churches where the fox tales of the Middle Ages have left their mark. The towering brick building once belonged to the Franciscan monastery beside it. Both church and monastery were built in the first half of the fourteenth century, and served as a center for the Franciscan order in the Baltic region until the Reformation drove the friars out of Lübeck as well. Art historian Miriam Mayer of St. Anne's Museum, which now administers the church building, equips me with a pocket flashlight before leading the way through the church building. The flashlight comes as a surprise. It is one o'clock in the afternoon, and daylight streams in through the high windows—but as we take a step down and continue amid a forest of small stone pillars, I see the point. It is dimly lit down here. The light doesn't reach as high as the small ceiling vaults, but with a flashlight you can see that the keystone in each vault contains a circular relief. They portray a wide variety of motifs—garlands of leaves, flowers, and mythical creatures. Eventually, the beam of light also illuminates the reliefs in which the fox appears.

They are in poor condition, which is hardly surprising considering that they are almost seven centuries old, dating back to around 1335. Nonetheless, you can work out what they are supposed to depict. Together, the three circular reliefs constitute a kind of comic strip about the fox. In the first image, he stands before four geese delivering a sermon. In one paw he holds a pilgrim's staff, a symbol of piety—but at the top of the next vault, my flashlight falls upon a new motif, showing the fox with one of the geese held between his teeth. So, the preacher has turned out to be a gluttonous fraud. In the third vault, he gets his just deserts. Two geese hold either end of a rope in their beaks, and together they pull the fox up on the gallows.

There is no question that, in this case, the fox symbolizes a bad priest or preacher, but the images are too old to have anything to do with Luther or Protestantism. They must be interpreted as a warning against traitors within the church, against priests who are dissolute and immoral—perhaps even heretical, and therefore spokesmen for the devil himself. Similar series of images involving foxes and geese, as well as other motifs in which the treacherous fox pretends to be religious, can be found in churches across much of Europe. Perhaps they may be seen as a variation on the wolf in sheep's clothing, the image used in the Bible to warn against false prophets. At any rate, it seems that the fox was often used as a symbol when people wished to criticize opponents within the church.

IN THE MID-TWELFTH CENTURY, the fox acquired the name Reinardus. The author who came up with the name was a monk in the Flemish city of Ghent, in modern-day Belgium, who wrote in Latin. The monk's epic poem was called *Ysengrimus* and much of it dealt with the conflict between the strong, greedy, simple-minded wolf Ysengrimus and small but sly Reinardus. There wasn't really a proper hero, since all the animals represented human failings, but Ysengrimus was the biggest fool of them all—and it was often Reinardus who ensured that the wolf got what was coming to him. Some of the episodes were directly inspired by Aesop's fables. Others betray the writer's more northern origin, because here we already find a tale about the fox tricking the wolf into fishing with his tail so that he gets frozen stuck in the ice. The author's real agenda seems to have been to comment on the internal affairs of the Catholic Church, and to poke fun at his enemies.

The fox Reinardus took on entirely new functions from the 1170s onward, when he became the protagonist in a collection of tales in verse that were first written in French, known as the *Roman de Renart*. The stories built upon the material from *Ysengrimus*, but now instead of dealing with church politics, they involved courtly life, law, and honor. The fox, the wolf, and the other animals are the foremost vassals of King Noble, the lion. One important event is the complicated affair between Renart and the she-wolf

Hersent, which starts out as run-of-the-mill adultery but ends in a rape—which is depicted pretty much as graphically as possible—and is much more explicit than in the later, northern European retellings. Ysengrin, the male wolf, turns up and happens to see the whole thing. Unreasonably enough, what ensues is largely about *his* humiliation and disgrace, and his unsuccessful attempts to seek redress through legal proceedings, rather than the she-wolf's experience of the event. One aspect of the story that was probably seen as comic by medieval readers is that Ysengrin only makes things worse for himself by airing his dirty laundry in public.

Roman de Renart parodies other courtly literature. Rather than being a knight living up to his ideals—infinitely bold, loyal, and so on—the protagonist Renart is a rascal who breaks all the rules, and that is precisely how he prevails. There are countless versions of *Roman de Renart*; rather than being a single coherent work, it is a patchwork of tales with the same cast of characters, written by different authors who built upon the version of the original writer. These stories became tremendously popular. One sign of their success is that the name Renart is even more firmly embedded in the French language than Mikkel is in the Nordic region. In medieval French, the protagonist is called *Renart le goupil*, or Renart the Fox—but nowadays, *goupil* has fallen out of use and the animal is simply called *renard*.

Reinardus traveled onward. With the advent of printed books, the sly fox went from strength to strength across northern Europe. The first translation into English (in prose, not poetry) was printed in 1481. The stories about Reynard the Fox, as he is called in English, were constantly repackaged so that they could be read as commentaries on politics, religion, morality, or social customs, and so that they reflected different points of view.

Even today, this particular tradition of stories about foxes is very much alive. Written tales about Reynard have continued to mutate and spread to this day. The Nordic variant, in which the fox became Mikkel, is just one of many branches. One version that reached a large audience was Johann Wolfgang von Goethe's High German retelling, *Reineke Fuchs*, first published in 1794. In more recent times, Roald Dahl's *Fantastic Mr. Fox* contained a fair amount of Reynard's character.

In the twentieth century, Reynard the Fox even came close to becoming a colleague of Snow White and Cinderella as the hero of a Disney animated film. Walt Disney himself was fascinated but concerned. "The whole central character is a crook. That's what I'm afraid of," he said. The project was shelved, but the characters that had already been drawn were recycled and later served as the starting point for the cast in Disney's animated *Robin Hood* in 1973. So if millions of children had their first encounter with England's most famous outlaw in the form of a fox, it's all down to Reinardus.

And he's responsible for more than that. We tend to think the red fox has a crafty look, and so we read-ily describe it with adjectives like cunning and sly, but I think that has more to do with the stories passed down to us from previous generations than our own experience of the flesh-and-blood animal.

A Fox Book

THE DOOR OF Herman H. J. Lynge & Søn's antiquarian bookshop in Copenhagen is locked. There's a window display with first editions of old books, and behind it I catch a glimpse of shelf after shelf of volumes, most of them leather-bound with gold lettering on their spines. At first, it looks deserted. Then, I spot movement. An elderly woman and a man with white hair and beard come into view, and there's a younger man too, perhaps their son. None of them shows any sign of planning to open up the shop, even though it's past the official opening time. After standing on tiptoe, and craning to the right and left in an effort to make eye contact with the people inside, I find a bell with a label beneath it: "Ring here." So I do. The elderly man comes and opens up at once, and the inside of the shop reveals itself to be an organized chaos of old books, not just on the overfilled bookshelves, but also in piles on chairs and tables, on the floor, and on either side of each step of the already narrow staircase that leads up to the second floor.

"Welcome," says the white-haired man.

"Thank you," I say. "I'm the guy who wanted to take a look at *A Fox Book*."

The younger man takes charge and points me toward the innermost corner of the room.

"You can sit here," he says as he clears away two long-stemmed glasses, which hold the dregs of something resembling rhubarb cordial or rosé wine from the end of a narrow table, where the heaps of books are forced to beat a temporary retreat. Here he puts down three books—one is fairly small, its light-brown leather cover worn smooth, while the other two are large, almost immaculate tomes.

"Is this the 1555 edition?" I ask, awestruck, as I point at the small, light-brown volume. The bookseller confirms that it is.

"Can I take a look inside?"

"Of course, be my guest."

I leaf through carefully. The book costs the equivalent of roughly ten thousand dollars. Even though its five-hundredth birthday is approaching, the yellowing pages are still intact, and if you're comfortable deciphering Gothic script, the text, in archaic Danish, is still easy to read. "A Fox Book, which is called Reinicke Foss in German / and is a wonderful and merry Book with many beautiful Stories / merry Rhymes / Examples / and lovely Illustrations / which has never before appeared in Danish / recently rendered in Danish by Herman Weigere, Citizen of Copenhagen."

The book I'm holding is the reason for my trip to Denmark. For it was here, in this book, that the fox that featured in so many legends was first called Mikkel. A man named Herman Weigere translated the long tale of the fox from German to Danish and replaced the German name of the main character, Reineke, with the more Danish-sounding Mikkel.

The story itself is in rhyme. It opens with a woodcut of two lions, with crowns on their heads, sitting on a throne—evidently the king and queen—with a crowd of animals gathered before them. The king of the animals has summoned his foremost noblemen to a meeting. Only the fox is not there. He has done so many wicked deeds that he doesn't dare show his face, and no sooner has the meeting begun than the accusations about him start to flood in.

One of them comes from the rooster, who says that the fox disguised himself as a monk and convinced the hens he had become so devout that he lived in poverty and abstained from eating meat. In this way, he tricked them into leaving the safety of the henhouse. The woodcut that illustrates the chapter about the tribulations of the chickens shows the fox standing on his hind legs in a monk's habit, with Catholic rosary beads in one paw. In the other, he holds a letter from the king commanding him to keep the peace—a letter that he claims inspired him to adopt his new, meat-free lifestyle. The rooster studies the letter from the king. In the background, we see the fox in his natural posture, on all fours, with a hen in his jaws.

After that, Mikkel is summoned to the court over and over again; sometimes he uses his cunning to wriggle out of going, but other times he has no option but to turn up, and in those cases he talks his way out of the most impossible situations. Whether he's fighting a duel against the stronger wolf or standing on the gallows with a noose around his neck, it is his silver tongue that saves him. The fox invents, lies, lures, bewilders, flatters, and boasts until his enemies are the ones that end up being killed or flayed alive by order of the king, or are forced to pretend that nothing has happened. Mikkel is ultimately appointed chancellor. In other words, the villain becomes the king's most important counsellor and representative. Fundamentally, *A Fox Book* is an amoral tale. Readers are invited to rejoice in the exploits of the self-centered and unscrupulous protagonist—and to roll their eyes at the folly of the world and the rulers who allow themselves to be tricked. This amorality is camouflaged by wrapping the poem itself up in plentiful moralizing explanations of the content, intended to give the impression that the book has an edifying purpose— because the story seemingly reveals all kinds of bad behavior that we are supposed to guard against.

It strikes me that *A Fox Book* is a bit like the fox-monk himself—its unprincipled core is disguised as a sermon.

OF COURSE, I'm not going to buy a book that costs ten thousand dollars. Those other two large volumes that the booksellers brought out, on the other hand... They're exclusive enough too, being one of just four hundred sets of a two-volume deluxe edition published in 1915 and 1923, which contains the original text of *A Fox Book* and all the illustrations, along with copious scholarly comments, notes, and glossaries. Swept away by the bibliophilic atmosphere, I cough up the two hundred or so dollars that the books cost and leave the store carrying several pounds of fox book, neatly packaged in bubble wrap and a cotton tote.

Long Nights

BACK HOME, there has been a light snowfall, and the fox sneaks alone through the lengthening nights. Any sighting of it is in black and white. On the very edge of the forest beside the meadow, I've set up three wildlife cameras. They are often triggered by the movement of a roe deer, a squirrel, a moose, a badger, a flock of birds, or swaying branches; only once in a while does the longed-for fox appear. In the November darkness, the fox's reflective eyes look like two ghostly, white lanterns when it turns to face the camera while it is in night-vision mode. A cat comes and urinates beside an old den with two openings and is captured in color in the daylight. Late that night, the spectral fox appears and sniffs at the cat piss before cocking its own hind leg and marking the same spot. But this is a rare high point. Generally speaking, I'm disappointed by how little insight the cameras offer me into the fox's life; there is clearly an art to placing the camera correctly that can take years to perfect.

In January, one fox chases another along the animal trail where one of the cameras stands, running at breakneck speed. The mating season is approaching. After the solitary weeks of fall, the foxes become intensely interested in each other as rivals and as partners, and the winter nights echo with yaps and screams. Some weeks after the chase, the wildlife camera picks up a fox that stands in the wood barking—something like *woof-woof-woof-woof*, but in a high, hoarse, birdlike tone. I hear the same sound one moonlit night as I sit freezing my nose off by the edge of the field. On none of these occasions do I hear any response, but my reading tells me that foxes use this sound to maintain contact and often bark back and forth as they draw closer to each other. The fox's bloodcurdling scream, which you may also hear in winter, is even more directly linked to the mating season. The foxes probably scream to attract partners. They also scream when they are fighting, and they make a tremendous racket while they're actually mating.

Estrus is triggered by the season—in other words, by changes in light and weather. Farther south in Europe, mating may occur as early as January, but up in the north, it usually takes place in February or March. The vixen is in heat for roughly three weeks, but is only receptive to fertilization for three days. That's when it must happen. The male fox watches over his partner as closely as he can while she is in heat. Even so, she may well mate with a neighbor or an itinerant fox, and that can result in a litter of cubs consisting of half-siblings with different fathers. Both vixens and male foxes spray more urine around during the mating season, as scent signals for other foxes. Now and then, you may see the parallel tracks of a pair of foxes walking together, or imprints in the snow that show they have been playing.

The courtship of foxes is described in detail by the Scottish zoologist David Macdonald. His 1987 book *Running With the Fox* contains wonderful eyewitness accounts of foxes' social lives in both captivity and freedom. A series of photographs shows two flirting foxes, circling around in the snow, pouncing on each other, rising up on their hind legs, and leaning against each other, jaws agape and ears laid back. "Their postures reveal an uneasy blend of playfulness and aggression," a photo caption reads. Elsewhere in the book, Macdonald describes the prelude to mating between a pair of foxes in a large enclosure. As the critical moment approached, the male fox followed hot on the heels of the vixen. If she slept, he would wander off restlessly but come back and check how she was doing at least every three minutes. He might also lie down to rest while she slept, as close as he was allowed, but he kept his eyes half-open at all times. If she was walking around, he dogged her footsteps. If he got too close, she would chase him off with gaping mouth and sharp sounds, but she gradually permitted more liberties—after a while, a paw on her rump was acceptable, but that remained the limit for now. As the male fox went about like this, utterly absorbed in his partner, a wild mood took hold of the four younger vixens in the enclosure, fully grown daughters from the previous year's litter. They mounted one another and even their mother and father, clinging fast and riding them, even when they met with active resistance. They ended up in fights. Play could tip over into genuine aggression in a matter of seconds. While two of the young vixens were fighting, a third sister seized the opportunity to mount one of the brawlers. But despite the general licentiousness in the enclosure in the hours before mating, only the dominant vixen was fertilized that winter.

That's often the way it is. Where foxes live in extended family groupings containing several adults—whether in captivity or in the wild—the dominant vixen is usually the only one to have cubs. David Macdonald's study indicated that male foxes showed no interest in the subordinate vixens. That may either be because they never came into heat, or else because they were prevented from signaling that they had. No one can say what holds the others back—whether it is the dominant vixen's behavior or perhaps the scents she emits.

Sometimes, even so, a subordinate vixen in a family group may come into heat, mate, and have young during the same spring as the dominant vixen. Given the family structure, where daughters often remain in the home range where they were born and belong to an extended family group, you might think there would be more likelihood of interbreeding caused by fathers mating with their daughters. Yet genetic testing of foxes that lived in a residential area on the outskirts of Bristol, England, told a different story. Although both male and female foxes sometimes did have young with their own offspring, it was very much the exception. And while subordinate members of the family group were often daughters of the dominant vixen, they rarely turned out to be the offspring of her partner—the dominant male. That may be because the vixen had a fling with another male in previous years, or it may be that she switched partners in the meantime, simply because her former partner died. Wild foxes don't live so very long.

THE MATING PROCESS itself is much the same as with dogs. When the vixen finally signals that she is ready, the male mounts her. His penis swells up inside her, locking them together for several minutes after he has ejaculated. This locking can sometimes persist for more than an hour. While their underparts are still connected, the male fox dismounts and lifts one leg over the vixen's rump, so that they end up standing back to back, the better to defend themselves against others if necessary. Mating dogs will end up standing in the same way—locked together but facing in opposite directions. In a short story called "The Dogs in Thessaloniki," author Kjell Askildsen used this posture as an unforgettable symbol of a painful marriage that lasted for years even after the love had died. Even for the dogs and foxes themselves, there seems to be an element of conflict in this kind of coupling. The behavior of the vixen suggests that the locking is painful. It's doubtful that the individual male fox has any control over what happens himself—I don't believe anyone knows for sure—but the prolonged coupling probably increases the likelihood that his genes are the ones that will fertilize the vixen's egg by literally barring the way for other suitors.

Feeding Time at the Zoo

AT ONE IN THE AFTERNOON on a fine February day, four or five little family groups of humans turn up at the gate of the fox's enclosure at the Bjørneparken zoo in Flå, northwest of Oslo. Before they let us in, the keepers tell us that the foxes are affected by the ongoing mating season. That means there's a risk they won't have much of an appetite and may not eat out of our hands, which is what we're here to experience. Admittedly, there's only one vixen—albeit sterilized—living here, and the male foxes she lives with are close family members: her three brothers and their common father. Yet still, the hormones rage. Now and then, wild foxes turn up outside the high, wire mesh fence.

Once we've passed through the two gates of the security barriers, we sit down in a semicircle, adults and children, our faces turned toward the young man who stands in the snow and explains the ritual we are about to undergo. His colleague hands out disposable gloves. We pull them on, and then a bucket filled with bloody scraps of meat is passed around. We each help ourselves to a piece of liver from a road-killed moose, while the five red foxes, which have now come wandering over from their resting places among the pines, circle around us. They scrutinize us with their guarded, golden-brown eyes, some tentatively, others grimly self-assured. They don't seem threatening. But nor do they make any attempt to ingratiate themselves; there are no imploring eyes or tilted heads—the foxes are simply trying to predict where the food will appear from and are ready to leap away if anyone makes a sudden movement or tries to grab them. We do as we are told, keeping the scraps of meat in our closed hand, which we hold near our body until the keeper counts one, two, three. Then we all stretch our hands out simultaneously and offer the foxes the opportunity to help themselves from a flat open hand, so that all of them will get some food and no fingers will accidentally end up in a fox's mouth.

The foxes have long, copper-red winter pelts. The longest fur belongs to the oldest fox here, who is father to the rest. Back in the day, he was bought from a fur farm. His daughter and three sons, all adult animals, are the offspring of a wild-born vixen who is no longer alive.

One of the young male foxes comes over and snaps up the blackish-red morsel of liver. As he cranes forward, he lays his ears back. Soon, he returns to lick the blood off my disposable glove, and through the rubber I feel the body heat from his soft tongue.

Two red foxes in their winter coats stand on their hind legs
and fight, jaws agape to threaten each other with their teeth.
Bjørneparken zoo, Norway, February.

Around us, minor confrontations arise as the foxes
get too close to each other; they signal through small
noises and posture, much of which resembles canine
language. Self-assured foxes stalk around on straight
legs, tails and ears pointing up. Scared or submissive
ones crouch low, ears and tails pointing down.

Just before our visit ends, the fur starts to fly
between the vixen and one of her brothers, and we
hear a series of noises that don't sound anything like
the barking of dogs, but more like agitated monkeys
or the cackling of large birds. Gekkering, I think. The
term, coined by David Macdonald to refer to this stut-
tering noise, was inspired by the German verb *keckern*.

Macdonald learned that word from the behavioral scientist Günter Tembrock, who kept red foxes at his laboratory in postwar East Berlin—where he developed detailed catalogs of their behavioral patterns and sound repertoire.

The vixen chases the male fox away from the feeding area. Over in the blueberry bushes, they rise up on their hind legs and lean their forepaws against each other's bodies, as if wrestling or dancing. No one gets hurt, but the mood seems tense. Their faces are close and both animals' jaws are agape, with rows of sharp teeth showing. The foxes stand in exactly the same posture as the ones Tembrock sketched and photographed in black-and-white more than sixty years ago.

The Man With the Foxes

GÜNTER TEMBROCK (1918–2011) discovered more about the red fox's behavior than any scientist before him. Among his colleagues in the field of animal behavior, he was known as "the man with the foxes." In 1948, as a young zoologist, he succeeded in setting up a behavioral research institute at Humboldt University of Berlin, in East Berlin's Soviet-occupied sector. The fact that he and the institute ended up working with foxes in particular was something of an accident. A red fox just happened to be the first animal they got their hands on, as he explained in a letter to the more senior behavioral scientist Konrad Lorenz.

The fox was a male cub they called Putzi. He was born in the wild in the spring of 1948 in Soviet-occupied Thuringia. Soon Putzi gained some companions; these foxes came to Tembrock not just from East Germany, but also Czechoslovakia and even remote parts of the vast Soviet Union. The Cold War had broken out. Humboldt University was located in the part of Berlin that had been incorporated into the East German state, the DDR—which was founded on October 7,

1949, with Günter Tembrock among its inhabitants. At that point, he already had six red foxes under his care. They moved into a specially equipped room at the university and, after some years of work there, Tembrock was ready to start publishing his findings. His catalog of the behavioral patterns of the red fox described how the animals walked, stood, ran, jumped, hunted, ate, defecated, rested, played, fought, and reproduced; it also provided a detailed overview of the body language and sound repertoire of the species.

Tembrock identified forty different sounds from the foxes in his laboratory, which he then grouped into a smaller number of main types. So the question posed by Norwegian comedy duo Ylvis had already been answered—almost sixty years before they made their international breakthrough with the song "The Fox (What Does the Fox Say?)." You'd almost think the Ylvis brothers had read their Tembrock. The foxes said "Oof-oof," Tembrock wrote in an attempt to convey the contents of his audiotapes, as well as "Hiiiiiiiiiiiii," and even "How-ow-ow-ow."

Tembrock's work with the tape recorder placed him at the vanguard of international developments. His analyses of the fox's voice made a pioneering contribution to the field of bioacoustics—the study of animal sounds. Nowadays, anyone at all can listen to Tembrock's foxes on the Animal Sound Archive website, along with thousands of other animal sounds in the collection he founded. In the 1990s, some British researchers produced a new analysis of the red fox's sound repertoire. They studied recordings of wild foxes and described the species' sounds less colorfully, but using newer, more technically advanced methods, and their findings largely overlapped with those of Tembrock. They found twenty distinct sounds. The foxes often combined these basic sounds when communicating with each other, or repeated them in sequences. As is the case with dogs and people, they probably modify their signals by varying exactly how the different types of sound are uttered—in other words, through differences in sound volume, pitch, duration, and so on.

Yet sound is only one small part of the foxes' language. The wealth of body language that Tembrock sketched in his neat line drawings allows foxes to signal moods such as playfulness, aggression, self-confidence, superiority, submissiveness, and fear, among others, as well as various combinations and transitional forms of all these. Even though there's a lot that resembles wolves and dogs, there are also differences. When the two foxes at the zoo went up on their hind legs in that belligerent dance of theirs, they didn't snarl like dogs—those menacing grimaces, in which upper lips are drawn back to bare the teeth, are simply not among the fox's facial expressions. Later work on other species of the dog family, which builds upon Tembrock's research, indicated that snarling is a specialty that evolved on the wolf's branch of the canid family tree after they split off from the foxes. Foxes have a different way of threatening with their teeth: they simply gape.

Body language and sounds are the signals that are easiest for us humans to observe. But the foxes themselves also use another channel to transmit and receive—a channel nature has poorly equipped us to register, because foxes—like dogs—live in a world of scent. For example, they show a striking interest in sniffing each other's snouts and hind parts, as well as urine and feces left by other foxes. The several characteristic sniffing postures Tembrock identified among foxes included one he called "violet sniffing." This does not refer to a particular interest in flowers but to the sniffing of the violet or tail gland, which lies on the upper surface of the fox's tail, roughly three inches from the root. The violet gland is visible from a distance as a darker area in the tail fur. It secretes sebum with a marked scent that is said to be reminiscent of violets. The fox also has scent glands beside its anal opening, on its face, and on its paws. No one knows much about the signals foxes send each other with these glands, but in many social situations, foxes engage in conspicuous tail-lashing—which does not entirely correspond to the wagging of a dog's tail—and when they do so, they are probably wafting scent messages as well as transmitting the visual signals that we so easily get hung up on. What's more, foxes use scent to communicate with other foxes that have not yet arrived. They spray urine and deposit feces in order to mark the boundaries of their territory, to attract partners in mating season, and to tag food they have saved for later, among other things. Sometimes, they perfume their feces with secretions from their anal glands, sometimes not. We must assume they have their reasons for this.

TEMBROCK'S FOXES LIVED in groups and generally interacted freely while the scientists observed, but all this happened in an environment that was far from natural. Some of the behavioral patterns Tembrock described were influenced by the fact that the animals were trying to live out their vulpine nature in surroundings that did not encourage it. They used their forepaws to scratch and dig at hard walls and floors, or the thin layer of bedding material. Tembrock observed that the male fox Jupp could become so absorbed in his fruitless labor that he would chase off his cubs if they came and disturbed him. Jupp also used to take scraps of meat with him to an area where the substrate on the floor was deep enough to allow him to hide the meat by shoving the bedding material on top of it. When he was kept in a cage with a smooth stone floor, he covered his scraps of meat with a big bone. The vixen called Fiffi often tried to hide her meat for later by sticking it under the edge of the water bowl, or she would try to fold the edge of the food bowl itself over the meat that it contained. The result was that she ended up pushing the whole thing around on the floor. The foxes were observed rushing around frantically with food in their mouth, hunting for a suitable hiding place—even though they generally had to settle for a poor solution, like a corner or a windowsill. One time, the staff found that one of the foxes had covered the milk bowl with hay. In short, they had a striking need to store food.

AFTER THE RESULTS of Tembrock's work with foxes began to appear, the history of his research took a peculiar turn. It seems that the powers that be in the East German government put their foot down. Around the time when the Berlin Wall was built in 1961, Tembrock's contributions on the international research front ceased. The wall was only part of the explanation, although it was bad enough in itself. Throughout the 1950s, people had been able to travel freely between East and West Berlin, and Tembrock used to meet fellow academics at conferences in the West, as well as publish in Western journals. Now he lost much of that contact. But there was more to it than that; Tembrock felt that he was being directly undermined. It wasn't just small problems, like letters failing to reach him, or books and audiotapes mysteriously vanishing from his office. Shortly after Tembrock was appointed professor, he was barred from supervising PhD students, which would usually have been a natural part of a university professor's job. The behavioral research under his leadership was shut down, and Tembrock was transferred to other duties. He believed certain individuals in the ruling party wanted to hamper his work. Tembrock held on to his university post as best he could—for example, by focusing on applied research into guide dogs for visually impaired people—and apparently he got by reasonably well. In the 1980s, many East Germans got to know him through a series of animal programs on TV, including, obviously, a long episode about the fox. Nonetheless, looking back at Tembrock's work in the postwar era, you can't help asking: Why on earth was fox research politically controversial?

Of course, foxes can symbolize people—like when they preach to the geese in church art, or trick the king in a book. Was that what the leaders of East Germany feared? They no doubt realized that humans were animals too. Perhaps it might be risky to let someone study the behavior of different animal species, and the way they interacted and formed groups, unless the work was securely anchored in the Marxist-Leninist doctrines of the ruling party. People might start getting ideas.

A more precise answer as to why studies of vulpine behavior might be seen as a threat probably lies in the school of behavioral biology that Tembrock subscribed to. In the postwar years, he was part of an international community of scientists who developed the discipline of ethology, which is the study of animals' natural behavior. This academic community included Nikolaas Tinbergen, Karl von Frisch, and Konrad Lorenz, all of whom went on to win Nobel Prizes. The ethologists were often interested in instincts, that is, innate behavioral patterns. Instinctive behavior is generally typical for the species concerned. It is triggered by particular stimuli, without the animal having to learn that it needs to behave in a particular way; so if, for example, you tap lightly on the ground with a pen or your fingertip in the vicinity of newly hatched chicks, they will come running over and start to peck for food for the very first time. If the chicks are with their mother, they peck where she pecks. More generally, ethologists were interested in the particular behavioral repertoires of the different species, which can encompass both typical instincts and behavior that must be learned and sometimes requires a lot of practice. The way foxes buried their food for later and the fact that they fought in an upright position were exactly the kind of things they took note of.

Ethologists, who were largely based in Europe, were involved in a long-running academic dispute with the American school of behavioral biology, behaviorism, which was more interested in learning than instincts and placed greater emphasis on the similarities between different species. The so-called behaviorists restricted themselves to working with a few tried-and-true research animals, such as rats and pigeons, whereas the European ethologists studied all kinds of different species—and Tembrock was for some years their fox specialist.

After Tembrock's death in 2011, the anthropologist Wulf Schiefenhövel delivered a blazing eulogy at Humboldt University. Schiefenhövel drew attention to the following explanation for Tembrock's difficulties: the prevailing ideology in the Eastern Bloc was that one could mold human beings however one wished. Our species has no fixed nature whatsoever, and if one could only alter society, it would also be possible to create an entirely new kind of human being. This was where the idea of a natural and partly innate repertoire of behavioral patterns in all species—the animal species' *nature*—came dangerously close to the issue of our own human nature. Humans were also an animal species, after all. So it was safer to stick to the belief that both we and other animals were blank slates, on which one could draw and write almost anything at all. This view held considerable sway in both the Soviet Union and the United States in the postwar years, Schiefenhövel pointed out. In the East, many relied on a simplistic interpretation of the work of Russian behavioral scientist Ivan Pavlov—the man who got dogs to drool as soon as a food bell rang. In short, they were keen to talk about what humans and other animals could learn, but to say as little as possible about the propensities they possessed from birth.

So perhaps it was this belief in humanity's almost infinite malleability that some felt was under threat from Tembrock's interest in the "species-typical behaviors" of foxes and other animals. Perhaps they feared the next step would be a behavioral catalog for humans, with contents they wouldn't much like. In other words, some readers may have interpreted Tembrock's reports about the red foxes Putzi, Fiffi, and Jupp in much the same way as earlier readers had interpreted the tales of Reineke and Mikkel—their protagonists might be foxes, but the actual topic of the stories was human nature.

A Successful Species

THE RED FOX'S behavioral repertoire and its lithe body add up to a recipe for success. Evolution has molded the fox into a flexible animal that can adapt to all manner of habitats and diets. This adaptability comes in especially handy now, in the age of humanity, because the red fox is among those fortunate species that largely benefit from our transformation of the landscape.

In Northern Europe, foxes are more numerous than ever. In Norway's case, the population growth is clearly reflected in hunting statistics. Between 1880 and 1932, fox bounties were paid out across most of the country because the fox was seen as a pest, and people were well paid for the pelts besides. Even so, only a few thousand foxes were caught each year. The record over the whole of this period was around 13,500 animals shot or trapped in 1904. Since the Second World War, the number has been consistently higher—hunters have often caught roughly twenty to thirty thousand animals per year, and a downturn in the 1980s, which was due to an outbreak of fox mange, proved temporary. There are good grounds to believe that the rise in the number of foxes caught by hunters is due to population growth.

One of the reasons why times have been good for the red fox since the Second World War is the growth in deer populations. All things considered, the fox has probably also benefited from the disappearance of the large carnivorans native to Scandinavia—the wolf, the Eurasian lynx, the brown bear, and the wolverine. These four species had been wiped out across most of Norway and Sweden by the middle of the twentieth century and remain scarce to this day. Although larger predators do abandon carcasses that can provide it with a meal, the fox also has to watch its back because the wolf and lynx are quite capable of killing it, either to rid themselves of a troublesome competitor or simply to eat it.

There are several more factors that may help explain why foxes have become so numerous. A warmer climate with less snow cover may make it easier for them to find food. Moreover, new forestry practices of clear-cutting large areas, introduced in the twentieth century, may have improved access to field voles. Growth in human populations and prosperity also provides opportunities for the fox in the form of food waste from homes and restaurants, as well as roadkill carcasses along the highways.

THE FOX IS A SECRETIVE ANIMAL. No one knows exactly how many individuals there are, either in

Norway or elsewhere. The population peaks in spring and early summer, after the year's litters have arrived. After that, in the ensuing year until the next breeding season, young and adult foxes alike die. Some are shot. Some are killed by other animals, or die of starvation and disease. Accidents in steep terrain or on thin ice presumably happen to foxes as they do to other species, and we know that some are run over by cars. And then spring comes around and the dead are once again replaced by large litters.

GIVEN THE EVER-EXPANDING FOOTPRINT that we humans are leaving on the planet, the winning strategy for other species is to adapt to life around us. Foxes succeed on this count thanks to their flexibility and their ability to exploit the resources in a changing landscape. But of course, everything is relative. Other carnivorans do even better. Domestic dogs and house cats each outnumber the red fox in Norway and the rest of the world. So although the fox's flexible life strategy is successful, it has proven even more farsighted to specialize in living with humans—by moving into our homes as privileged guests, indeed, as members of the household. After all, humans control an ever-increasing share of the food available on the planet. So the animal species whose populations are booming are the ones we feed, not just pets but also livestock—such as chickens, farmed salmon, sheep, pigs, and cattle.

WHEN I RAISE my binoculars to check what is moving out on the meadows or along the edge of the forest, it often turns out to be a cat. That's always a disappointment. Not because I have anything against cats—they can be fun to watch—but a cat is nothing to write home about. It's a different matter entirely to see a sight as rare as a fox on the edge of the woods, a wild animal out hunting.

Wildness is one of the qualities I particularly value in the fox. In a way, it is wilder than other wildlife. The red fox does not owe its existence to game management, population targets, and hunting quotas—unlike the valuable moose and deer, or the ever-controversial larger carnivorans. The fox largely survives *in spite of* our plans and regulations, like an outlaw, so I see it as a symbol of freedom and independence.

In many places, landowners and hunters do their utmost to get rid of the fox. Elsewhere, they couldn't care less. The fox gets by either way. And in a world where we humans have seized control of far too much and left far too little room for the other species with whom we share the planet, *that* is good to see.

The Cousin on the Crags

THE SUCCESS OF THE RED FOX sometimes causes problems for other wild species, especially where the fox has expanded into new habitats. In a transition zone between forest and tundra in the northernmost part of Norway, for example, game wardens employed by the government shoot as many red foxes as they can in a bid to save the eggs and chicks of the tiny, local population of the lesser white-fronted goose—a species that is under threat of extinction globally. Similarly, the red fox can be a danger to its cousin, the Arctic fox. This species is still abundant in some parts of the Arctic, but the Scandinavian population is endangered. I have never met one while hiking in the mountains. After visiting the Bjørneparken zoo and feeding the red foxes there, my son and I hopped in the car and drove up into the highlands to have a close encounter with the Arctic fox as well. At Langedrag Nature Park, which lies just below the tree line, the snow was deep. Here too you could come and meet the foxes inside a spacious enclosure.

Two young Arctic foxes called Jesper and Jonatan, in their winter camouflage of snow-white fur,

An Arctic fox in its winter coat, hoping for a treat.
Langedrag Nature Park, Norway, February.

ran around making mischief. One of them grabbed
a woolly mitten from the hand of a boy in our party,
aged maybe eight, then dashed off with the mitten
in his mouth—and with his brother hot on his heels.
The mittenless lad took it in stride. Jesper and Jonatan
shared their enclosure with a red fox the same age as
them called Kasper, who was bigger and stronger, as
red foxes tend to be. Now he came bounding up to see
what all the fuss was about. Kasper stole the mitten
from his white-pelted pals, then ran away from them
to hide his treasure in the snow. With an apologetic

gesture, the keeper explained to the boy's parents that the mitten was unlikely to be found until spring.

THE ARCTIC FOX is more rounded in appearance than the red fox. Its ears are shorter. The same goes for its snout, and the angle of its forehead is steeper. In the harsh landscapes where the Arctic fox thrives, it can excavate enormous den systems with nearly a hundred entrances, and the areas around these residential complexes tend to be greener than elsewhere because the earth has been fertilized by the inhabitants' droppings for generations. Some of these ancient dens in Norway may have been inhabited for millennia. If we're to believe Günter Tembrock, who acquired a pair of Arctic foxes that were born at Moscow Zoo in 1956, the species' social behavior is very similar to that of the red fox. For example, the Arctic fox vixen he studied also rose up on her hind legs in playful wrestling matches with her partner, and both animals showed their teeth by gaping at each other.

Naturally enough, the fur of the Arctic fox is particularly dense and warm, and that made the animal a highly sought-after prey for fur trappers in days gone by. There are two color variants of this species: white fox and blue fox. White foxes, which are the more common of the two in the wild, switch between their white winter coat and a summer coat that is mostly brown, but in striking contrast to the paler underside.

The blue fox is a rarer variant. It has a grayish winter coat that can be perceived as blue. In summertime, the blue fox's coat is a fairly uniform brown color. In the wild, white and blue foxes reproduce freely with each other.

The Arctic fox's domain is the tundra, the treeless landscape that takes over from the forests in the highlands and the Far North. The species occurs in similar terrain all the way around the North Pole, in Russia, Canada, and Alaska, as well as on Iceland, Greenland, and other smaller islands. In total, the population is large and thriving. On Svalbard, I once met an Arctic fox that stood staring at me from a distance of mere yards in the middle of a highway. (The species is common on Svalbard.) On the Scandinavian Peninsula, however, it became rare after it was hunted intensively for its fur. Even though hunting was banned more than a century ago, the populations never really recovered. One of the reasons for this has been competition from the red fox. For wild animals, life is a struggle, of course, and conditions rarely allow for the idyllic coexistence of the fox species that we saw among the well-fed, young animals at the nature park.

Put simply, the Arctic fox's expertise lies in being the fox wherever conditions are too cold and barren for the red fox. In environments that are otherwise suitable for both species, the red fox will generally outcompete, scare off, or even kill its smaller relative.

Over several decades, red foxes have established themselves in former Arctic fox territory. In some places, they have taken over ancient Arctic fox dens. Above the tree line, the red fox is mostly found along highways and near holiday cabins, probably because it benefits from food waste. So one of the ways in which we humans pose a threat to the Arctic fox is by luring the red fox up into the mountains.

Climate change is another threat. For the Arctic fox, it will be catastrophic if the boom-and-bust cycle of the lemming population, with recurring "lemming years," comes to a halt. Lemmings and other voles are the Arctic fox's most important prey, and the lemming population in the tundra landscape peaks every few years. In such boom years, you'll see live and dead lemmings everywhere, and these lemming years are the times when Arctic foxes succeed in raising plenty of cubs. Scientists fear that climate change may make lemming years rarer and less abundant. There have been some signs that they are becoming more irregular in Scandinavia, and this may be one of the reasons why the Arctic fox is having difficulties in the region.

A warmer climate also means that the red fox can thrive farther north and higher up in the mountains, of course—driving the Arctic fox into retreat. For now, it is difficult to distinguish between the impact of climate change on animal life and the more local effects of human activity and our food waste. Eventually, the warmer climate will probably enable the forest to spread farther north and into the highlands, and forest animals such as the red fox will undoubtedly follow. Thus, ongoing climate change poses an existential threat to polar climate specialists such as the Arctic fox.

AT THE TURN OF the millennium, the Scandinavian Arctic fox population dipped to its lowest level, at around fifty adult animals. Since then, things have improved. In Norway alone, there are now roughly three hundred adult Arctic foxes, thanks to a program in which biologists began to breed cubs in captivity and then release them into the wild. They get a jump start in the form of automatic feeding stations, which have entrances too narrow for red foxes. With these strategies, the biologists have managed to reestablish the Arctic fox, even in areas where there are also red foxes, and without any systematic culling of the Arctic fox's larger relative. These results may indicate that scientists still have a lot to learn about the relationship between the two species. Perhaps the Arctic fox isn't quite as helpless in the face of the red fox as they had thought, and perhaps it is better placed to compete once it has a large and well-established population in an area. At any rate, the future prospects of the Arctic fox in Scandinavia appear to be brighter today than twenty years ago. Perhaps there is hope after all, even for the cousin on the crags.

Quarantine

IN TOPSY'S FIRST SUMMER, our puppy was supposed to come along on a trip to Sweden. It turned out that she needed to have her own doggy passport, with Norwegian and EU flags on the front. Inside the passport, there had to be three stamps and the signature of a veterinary surgeon, who certified that Topsy had undergone a special preventive course of deworming treatment—because if that wasn't sorted out, we risked not being able to take our dog back home to Norway. A few cases of an intestinal parasite called fox tapeworm or *Echinococcus multilocularis* had been detected in Sweden, and the Norwegian government was extremely keen to keep it out of the country. Fox tapeworm is widespread across large areas of the northern hemisphere and is especially common in foxes, although dogs and cats may also be infested. While it does little serious damage to either wild or tame carnivorans, it *is* harmful to humans. Human infection is fairly rare, but ingestion of fox tapeworm eggs via the excrement of infected animals—after touching a dead animal, say, or picking contaminated berries—may lead to a serious disease that can, at worst, prove fatal.

Over recent years, GPS tagging of red foxes has revealed that they sometimes roam hundreds of miles. So it goes without saying that they often cross national borders, which makes you wonder how effective it is to combat fox tapeworm with stamps in pet passports. I presume the parasite will make its way to Norway sooner or later. A foxhunter in my own neighborhood tells me that he earns several hundred kroner per fox carcass from the Norwegian Veterinary Institute, whose staff examine the intestines of the shot fox to make sure that they'll know whenever the fox tapeworm does arrive.

THIS IS PRECISELY how many people know the fox: as a bearer of contagion. The most important reason for this is rabies, the gruesome viral condition that is also known as mad dog disease because it makes both humans and animals aggressive and unpredictable. The rabies virus is mostly transmitted through saliva and can infect all kinds of mammals, although we humans most often contract it from dog bites. The disease has long been feared—a legal text on clay tablets from Mesopotamia (modern-day Iraq) dating back nearly four thousand years details the fines payable by owners of rabid dogs that have bitten and killed another person. The virus attacks the nervous system, altering behavior. Patient histories old and new make for terrifying reading. Here's one account of a rabies-stricken man from England in 1809:

> the teeth and gums of the upper jaw were constantly exposed, and frothy saliva ran out at the sides of his mouth—he begged me to kill him at once; stamped on the floor with violence, became furious, and could scarcely be held by the attendants. He was now confined on the bed with a strait-waistcoat—he wished to be confined when it was proposed—he now attempted to *kick* and *bite* every one who came near him.

It's enough to make you suspect that rabies served as inspiration for those legends of werewolves and vampires. The bite of a diseased animal—or indeed, human—does in fact lead to a terrifying, bestial transformation. The infected person may remain symptom-free for quite some time, but when the disease finally breaks out, death occurs within a matter of days.

One reason why rabies is so hard to control is that the virus is transmitted by wild animals. In 1580, for example, red foxes were said to have dug up the carcass of a pig that had died of rabies near Frankfurt, Germany. The foxes caught rabies. They bit each other and people, causing many to get sick and die. The solution to the problem was a large-scale foxhunt in the affected area. However, of all the wild animals in Europe, the wolf was the species most notorious in earlier times for spreading mad dog disease. Rabid wolves become extremely aggressive. Unlike their healthy peers, they may well attack people—indeed, the disease is probably a major reason for the wolf's bad reputation.

Toward the end of the nineteenth century, fear of rabies diminished in Europe. French chemist Louis Pasteur developed a vaccine, which could also be administered as a preventive measure after a person had been bitten by a suspected carrier but before they had become sick. Around roughly the same time, the disease disappeared in many parts of the world. The reasons for this are not entirely clear, although in many countries, the authorities had ownerless dogs put down. Dog owners were also ordered to muzzle their dogs, and to place them in quarantine if they were taken across a national border. At the same time, wolf numbers were on the decline.

Rabies has been absent from the Scandinavian Peninsula since the nineteenth century, and the British Isles became free of the disease early in the twentieth. The rest of the European continent, however, had a very different experience. A major new rabies outbreak started around the end of the Second World War, an outbreak that would last several decades, and this time the red fox was the main carrier. It has been

claimed that the outbreak started in Poland; the virus
may have benefited from the explosion in game populations in areas that were abandoned by most people
for a time because of warfare. At any rate, roaming
foxes spread the virus in waves across Central and
Western Europe, typically at a rate of twelve to thirty-
seven miles per year. The contagion died out when
fox populations became sufficiently sparse, whether
through disease or because foxes were shot on a
massive scale and gassed in their dens. But it proved
difficult to get the better of the fox. The strategy of
eliminating them only had a lasting effect in areas
where the landscape formed a natural bottleneck—
such as southern Jutland, by the border between
Germany and Denmark. Here, the Danes repelled
repeated rabies invasions between 1964 and 1982. Fox
bounties in the border area and den gassing reduced
the fox population by perhaps 80 percent in a zone
that extended a few dozen miles from the border into
Denmark. In the rest of Europe, however, it turned out
that much more lenient measures were most effective
in the long run. The solution was to vaccinate foxes.

Swiss scientists were the first to attempt a large-
scale vaccination campaign. From the summer of 1978,
a wave of contagion swept from the area around Lake
Geneva and up through the Rhône valley—until then
rabies-free. On October 17 of the same year, police
officers and foresters familiar with the area went into
action, armed with polystyrene boxes full of chicken

heads. A capsule of rabies vaccine had been inserted beneath the skin of each head, and one by one these pieces of medicated bait were hidden beneath the vegetation along the trails and roads leading up the valley. Helicopters were used to distribute the chicken heads in steep, snow-covered areas high up on the sides of the valley. The experiment was a success. The wave of contagion halted at Monthey, where the Rhône valley curves. The Swiss went on to use this method in valley after valley. By 1990, the foxes of Switzerland had received more than 1.3 million chicken heads—and better health in the bargain.

The chicken heads were effective. At the same time, though, they were awkward to work with, and in the early 1980s, German scientists came up with an alternative—the Tübingen fox bait, which was simply fish meal mixed in fat. Machines could then encase the vaccine capsules in tempting bait. Cheap, mass-produced wildlife vaccines helped country after country to declare themselves free of fox-borne rabies. The disease is found sporadically among Arctic foxes in polar regions, and they occasionally bring the infection to Svalbard when they roam across the sea ice in winter. The red fox, however, has been liberated from the disease over large areas. Most people can enjoy the sight of the red robber without fearing that it could bring mad dog disease into the neighborhood—yet another reason to count ourselves lucky that we invented vaccines.

A Natural Experiment

THE MANGE EPIDEMIC that broke out on the Scandinavian Peninsula while I was a child in the 1970s served as a large-scale natural experiment, and a unique opportunity for scientists to study the fox's impact on small-game populations.

For the red foxes of Norway and Sweden, mange was a catastrophe that can best be compared with the Black Death that ravaged humanity in the fourteenth century. Fox numbers plummeted by well over half, and the cause was a skin parasite that goes by the Latin name of *Sarcoptes scabiei*. It is also known as the scabies mite, because a mite is what it is—a tiny, eight-legged relative of the spider. And this particular mite is so tiny that it is barely visible without a magnifying glass. The scabies mite burrows just beneath the outer layer of the skin, then lays eggs, and, as any person who's ever been infected with scabies can tell you, it itches like hell. Scabies in humans is caused by a variant of the mite that specializes in living in human skin, and which can be transmitted from person to person. This irksome disease has existed since time immemorial. The mite that attacks foxes, however, is a different variant, and it causes a disease known as mange. It specializes in living beneath the skin of foxes and other predatory mammals, and causes only temporary irritation to humans who have come into contact with infected animals.

Fox mange was unknown in Norway and Sweden until the 1970s. As a result, the foxes there had no resistance to the disease, which explains why they were hit so hard when it eventually arrived. The infected foxes developed rashes and matted fur, followed by extensive hair loss, sores, and scabbing. Eventually, they stopped eating, becoming thin and emaciated. In the vast majority of cases, the disease led to death.

BUT EVERY CLOUD has a silver lining—the mange outbreak in the Scandinavian Peninsula offered a unique insight into the red fox's impact on the species it hunts. The most detailed studies were carried out at Grimsö Wildlife Research Station, which is located in a landscape of coniferous forest and bogland in inland Sweden at roughly the same latitude as Stockholm and Oslo. By the time mange reached this area in 1982, scientists had already been keeping count of foxes and their most important prey for a number of years. Each spring, they would set traps for field and bank voles, check all known den locations to see whether the foxes had had a litter, and record obser-vations of foxes and other game, such as mountain hares, roe deer, and various grouse species—the black grouse, the western capercaillie, and the hazel grouse.

Mange took such a toll on the fox population in the Grimsö area that the impact lasted for the rest of the decade. The number of litters did not recover until around 1990. Populations of field and bank voles, the foxes' most important prey in this area, turned out to be unaffected. There were roughly as many voles in the years before and after the mange outbreak; this is probably because they reproduce so quickly that the foxes' predations make no difference. However, the mountain hare populations rocketed in the 1980s when the fox population was lower. The same went for grouse. These are larger animals that reproduce more slowly and are less numerous than voles. The scientists' findings indicated that foxes caught so much small game that that they contributed to keeping populations down. Roe deer also had more luck raising their fawns when fox populations were low.

Hunting statistics showed that more hares, capercaillies, black grouse, and hazel grouse were shot when foxes were scarce. Pine marten populations also rose. That may be because either the fox previously killed a lot of pine martens or because the two species competed for food. As it ended, the natural experiment confirmed that the fox can certainly eat

enough small game to make an impact, because once
the mange outbreak abated and fox populations were
restored, the populations of many small-game species
declined once more.

THE MANGE EPIDEMIC ebbed out in the 1990s. Foxes
became numerous once again as they and the scabies mite reached a kind of uneasy equilibrium. The
disease didn't go away, but it did become less deadly,
whether because the surviving foxes were more resis-
tant or the parasite had evolved into a form that did
less harm to the host animal. It is now more common
than it used to be to find foxes that have been infected
but have not developed the disease. The current situation is similar to what we see on the European
continent and in the British Isles, where the disease has a permanent presence, with local outbreaks
occurring from time to time.

People have a tendency to seek meaning in everything that happens. It may be tempting to interpret fox
mange as a kind of punishment—nature's response
to an abnormally high fox population, say—but I'm
not sure life is as simple as that. The fox population
in Scandinavia was undoubtedly denser when mange
broke out than it had been a hundred years before,
and it can be easier for disease and parasites to spread
when population density is high. On the other hand,
much of the Scandinavian Peninsula consists of

barren landscapes, where foxes will always be more dispersed than in Southern Europe. In reality, no abnormal conditions are required to ensure the spread of a disease like mange. Nature is brutal. More than half of all species apparently live as parasites, so it is extremely common for small species like the scabies mite to exploit a far larger species like the fox.

Underground

DURING THE SPRING, I inspect old dens in the hope of finding out where one of this year's litters is on the way, so that I can be on the spot when the cubs emerge blinking into the daylight. In several places, there are fresh signs of digging beside the den entrance. It usually turns out to have been a busy badger, as revealed by a pawprint with five toes rather than the fox's four, or by the distinctive trench the badger digs that leads away from the den entrance, or by debris from its tireless efforts to fit out the den with moss, grass, or leaves. But there are a few places that look promising, where it seems a fox may have been at work. Outside the entrance, there's a bit of soil, rubbish that has recently been cleared out of the den. The pawprints in the loose soil are unclear but may indicate that it is indeed a fox that has been digging here, and that I'm on the right track. Whether a fox mother uses an old den or digs a new one, a spot of renovation is often in order before she settles down to give birth.

I CAN'T SEE what's happening underground, but I do know that the tunnel dug by the vixen slopes down from the entrance quite sharply. Only a few yards in does she reach the birthing chamber. From there, one or more tunnels usually lead to alternative exits. During the last few days before the birth, the vixen spends most of her time in the den, while her partner comes to deliver food for her, leaving it by the entrance. The cubs are born fifty-two to fifty-three days after mating—many are born in April.

You can find videos of fox births on the internet, filmed with night cameras in the subterranean darkness of wild vixens' dens. The fox mother gives birth alone. The efficient way she bites through the umbilical cord and removes the fetal membrane that usually coats each cub reminds me of the time when, as a teenager, I got to see our family dog give birth, because I happened to come home from school at just the right moment. The same thought strikes me now as then: what instincts! The mother knows exactly what needs to be done, even though she may be giving birth for the first time and has never seen another vixen give birth.

The cubs weigh around three-and-a-half ounces at birth. They are blind and helpless, and in their earliest days they cannot retain heat themselves, so two or three days pass before the mother can even leave the den. If her partner is late arriving with supplies, she will go to the entrance of the den and bark sharply. Inside, she is kept busy suckling and tending to the little ones. They urinate and excrete only when she licks their bellies, and the vixen keeps the den clean by eating all their bodily waste.

Between times she sleeps. Fox mothers that were observed in captivity spent more than 70 percent of their time asleep in the days and nights immediately after the birth, although that sleep was broken up into short naps of around ten minutes. That's also what I remember from the first night after my childhood dog had puppies. Mother and pups lay in a basket in my room, and no sooner would I drop off to sleep than one of the puppies would begin to squeak, because it had slipped off its mother's teat or lost contact with her body heat. Somewhere in the forest, the fox cubs whimper in very much the same way. Perhaps it's happening inside one of the dens I know about.

IN THEIR THIRD WEEK of life, the cubs open their eyes. For fox cubs living sheltered in the subterranean world their mother has made for them, there is little to see, but down in the darkness, they begin to develop a certain independence. At last, their legs are able to bear the weight of their small bodies. As soon as they are up on all fours, the cubs start to pick on each other. After a few days, these attacks develop into rather brutal fights. The cubs battle for status, for their position in the hierarchy of the litter, and this really is a matter of life and death because the highest-status cubs eat first—so if food is scarce, those that are lowest on the ladder may starve. The mother does not get involved.

She leaves the cubs to settle their differences among themselves, and around the eighth week, the aggression abates, since the ranking among the cubs is now fully established. This is the advantage of establishing a pecking order—not just for the winners but for the losers too. After all, they don't need to fight so often. Down in the darkness, the cubs also begin to play— almost as soon as they start to fight properly. They play alone and they play with each other. Little signals distinguish play fights from genuine aggression, reassuring the opponent that this is a game, not a threat, although it could well be that even play helps the siblings to work out who it may be worth challenging and who must simply be allowed to dominate.

A FEW DAYS AFTER getting up on their feet, the cubs set about exploring the rest of the den system. At the age of around four weeks, they usually take their first peek outside, and this is roughly the point at which the mother starts giving them solids. Unlike wolves— and some domestic dogs—foxes don't help their young by regurgitating half-digested food for them. At around two months, they start to be weaned off their mother's milk, but long before then, she begins to sleep away from the cubs, only returning the den to suckle them and deliver other food. The cubs spend increasing amounts of time out in the open air in the vicinity of the den entrance. While their parents hunt or rest, they are left to their own devices. To start off with, they are inquisitive and naive, so anyone who is lucky enough to know the location of an active den and takes care to approach cautiously and sit down quietly could get a chance to enjoy the sight of little foxes at play outside the den.

Early in May, the doubt crept up on me. No matter how much I scouted and lay low, I saw no adult foxes heading to or from the dens. The cubs showed no sign of peeking out. It was starting to look as if all the vixens in the area had managed to hide out in dens I didn't know about. Rumors of a well-used fox's den beneath a barn tempted me to make several morning trips out there; the best observation point proved to be a car stationed in the parking spot right beside a bus stop. Morning-weary cyclists and bus passengers looked at me in puzzlement as I sat there, keeping watch with my cup of coffee and binoculars, and in quiet moments after the bus had carried everyone away, I felt as if I were in some TV cop show—my stakeout partner could turn up any second, knocking on the car door with warm donuts and a cynical quip. Over by the barn, I saw a couple of the usual suspects: the badger returned from his night patrol and vanished under the barn, and a cat strutted around in the morning sun. But I called off this operation too in the end, because the only fox I spotted on these strange mornings showed no sign of having any business in the old den beneath the barn.

A Den of Thieves

WHEN AT LAST I found myself sitting beside a den inhabited by fox cubs, full of anticipation and cloaked in a green-and-brown camouflage sheet, with only the upper half of my face poking out, I was hampered by an unexpected problem: people. A woman with a white dog came walking toward me along the path just below, talking on her phone. With some effort, I freed my hands from the unfamiliar camouflage sheet, pulled the hood off my head, and did my best to look harmless, even though I was irritated to be disturbed like this.

"Hey, listen. I've come to what I think must be a fox's den," she said into her phone. "And there's a man sitting here in camouflage gear, so I think I'd better make myself scarce."

Her dog crouched flat on the ground and tugged on its leash as it tried to get to what was, indeed, the home of a litter of fox cubs—which had scattered birds' feathers, plastic bags, and other debris across the ground over a large area around the entrance. I smiled as amiably as I could. The dog owner backed off in the direction she'd come from, dog in tow and an interrupted conversation in her hand.

I shouldn't really have been surprised that there was plenty of outdoors activity here. One of the major hiking trails in Oslo's Nordmarka forest ran so close to the fox's den that voices were frequently audible through the spruce trees. An unmarked side-branch of the trail passed between the two entrances to the den. Traffic on this offshoot had probably increased lately, because someone had hidden an orienteering checkpoint in the bushes just beside it, and that checkpoint was the reason I'd heard about the cubs in the first place—it was an orienteering enthusiast who'd found them. She went straight back home, fetched a camera and camouflage net, and then posted a wonderful video clip of fox cubs at play online. A mutual friend saw the film and tipped me off, so here I sat now, cowering every time anyone came past.

THE ORIENTEER with the camera was called Helen. She kindly offered to show me the way to the den, and we met on the edge of the forest on a fine morning in mid-May. Even before we reached our destination, a stone's throw away from the den itself, we came across some wide-eyed cubs. At the very instant we found them, we also heard a voice that I initially thought must be a person calling out, but was probably an adult fox warning its young. At any rate, the cubs withdrew to the den. By the time we had settled down at our observation posts up a steep slope, the area was deserted apart from a lone cub that wandered around beside one of the entrances. Perhaps it had been on its own and hadn't heard the alarm. Now it sunned itself in a bright patch on the rocky knoll above the entrance to the den, scratched its cheek and ear—just like Topsy does—and uttered a kind of whimpering bark that I took to mean it was nagging its siblings to come back out and play, or perhaps these barks were a plea for its parents to come with some food. After a while, the little fox got up and stalked the blackbird that was hopping around on the ground, unconcerned, then it headed into the hollow beneath the knoll where the den entrance was. It returned again with what looked like the heel of a loaf of bread and lay down to gnaw on it. Then it wandered down into the den and vanished, leaving the area outside empty and quiet; not much else happened until Helen whispered that she had to go to work and I was left sitting there alone.

THE SUN CLIMBED higher in the sky. The patches of sunlight wandered across the forest floor. A pair of great spotted woodpeckers flew to and from their nest in a dead tree, and one of them started to search for food on the ground a couple of yards away from where I sat. Now and then, one, two, or three fox cubs would peek out down below. They seemed tentative and cautious to start off with and jumped at any sudden noises, but even though their hearing was sharp, their ability to sort impressions didn't seem very well developed. Gusts of wind in the treetops scared the little foxes more than the noises I let slip when I moved around up on the slope. Left undisturbed, they slowly began to let their guard down. Their play was quiet; what noise they made did not carry up to me. They leaped on each other and rolled around, and a few times, I saw one cub mount another, as if they were mating. Most of the time, the little foxes seemed to be on good terms. But once, I saw a relatively big cub repeatedly attack a smaller littermate, even though the little one just cowered and tried to get away.

Some twigs blocked my view of the fox cubs. What's more, I was too far away to get any good pictures; so in a quiet moment, I took out a plastic container of unsalted dried fish, the kind sold as doggy snacks. With some effort, I had chopped these chewy, foul-smelling treats into tiny pieces back home, and now, one by one, I threw the morsels onto the slope that led down to the den. I had qualms about doing this—neither party benefits when wild foxes become too trustful of people, so although fox cubs may be hungry and injudicious enough to let themselves be fed by hand, it is best not to do it. Scattering the treats on the slope was my compromise. A little before one in the afternoon, no fewer than six cubs appeared at the same time, but the buzzing of a small aircraft made them all jump, and two of the cubs chose to seek shelter underground. The four remaining foxes had just begun to wander slowly in my direction, perhaps attracted by the smell of dried fish, when the forest echoed with the sound of heavy footfalls and panting— a jogger on the trail. I cursed under my breath, and the cubs dashed back toward the den—but ended up sitting huddled together between the trail and the den opening, looking up at the jogger who stood before them, back toward me. "Hi there," he greeted the little foxes in a surprised voice, before running onward. Not until the man had gone did the last cubs vanish underground.

It was past one when an adult fox came storming onto the scene with a dead squirrel in its jaws. The cubs swarmed up from the den and flocked toward the adult, whining and wagging their tails, and this time, I counted a grand total of nine. One snapped up the squirrel and bolted into the forest. No one ran after it, which probably meant that the squirrel-snatcher was the undisputed leader of the litter—because young foxes reportedly fight over food with "astonishing savagery." The adult fox disappeared as swiftly as it had come. The cubs that hadn't gotten any squirrel started to disperse over the terrain, and several came my way. Now I noticed how stark the developmental differences between the siblings were—some were much larger than others, and the larger ones had redder coats than their smaller siblings. The ones that had spent part of the morning outside the den were apparently the smaller animals. Could it be that hunger

gave them no rest if their bigger, stronger littermates took the lion's share of the food? At any rate, the fox cubs began to sniff their way up the slope toward the dried fish. It was a struggle for them to chew the tough morsels, but once they'd succeeded, they were keen for more. Fortunately, what little wind there was blew toward me. I tried to move only when the foxes' attention was elsewhere and froze if they looked toward me or seemed nervous. Up they came. As I sneaked out my camera and began to snap away, it clearly dawned on them that something was stirring up on the hill, but they didn't run away. The dried fish was worth the risk.

Red fox cubs near the den.
Nordmarka forest, Oslo, Norway.

IN ADDITION TO the entrance beneath the rocky knoll, there was another one between the tree roots on the forest floor, perhaps ten yards away, just below the slope I was sitting on. The cubs went out and in through both. They also constantly crossed the flat clearing between the entrances and the hiking trail. Later in the afternoon, as the cubs were taking a nap underground, I became aware of an adult fox slinking among the spruce trees at the far end of the clearing. Looking in my direction, it walked back and forth a few times before vanishing. It probably sensed I was there and abandoned its plans to visit the cubs. The time had come to pack up and leave the fox family in peace.

A LITTER OF NINE is on the large side for a single vixen. It's unusual for vixens to give birth to that many, and it's probably difficult for a mother to raise many more cubs than she has teats—most often, six. If one vixen was the mother of this entire litter, she probably had plenty of help. On the very first day, I saw two adult foxes near the den. The suspicious fox sneaking among the spruces was a beautiful copper-red, with a marked white tip to its tail. The coat of the fox that had come running up with the squirrel earlier in the day, on the other hand, was more straw-yellow in color, and it had very little white on its tail. Both turned out to be vixens. Perhaps the two of them had given birth to litters, each in their own chamber within the den system, and were bringing up the cubs together. Or perhaps one vixen had birthed a record-breaking litter and was able to get by thanks to the other vixen's help. Without any solid reason for it, I caught myself assuming that the watchful copper-red vixen was the older and more experienced of the two.

The relationship between the adult vixens in a family group can be strained during the breeding season. The dominant vixen often prevents subordinate vixens from reproducing. And if they *do* manage to conceive, they may have problems with the pregnancy or rearing their litter. It isn't uncommon for vixens in captivity to kill their own cubs shortly after giving birth if they live in close quarters with a higher-status vixen—and this happens even if the vixens are in separate cages. Some type of signal from the dominant vixen, whether in the form of scent, sound, or something else, evidently causes so much stress to the subordinate vixens that they can end up utterly failing as mothers. Where vixens mingle freely in larger enclosures, people have also observed that the dominant vixen can subject competing vixens to intense bullying campaigns during the breeding season. Perhaps they are trying to prevent an extra litter because it would compete for local food resources as well as help from the male fox. The dominant vixen may even recruit the failed mother as a babysitter. David Macdonald reports one case in which a subordinate vixen lost her newborn litter—after being stressed into behavior that could be described as gross neglect—and ended up suckling the cubs of the dominant vixen. The bullying behavior of the dominant fox mother can also be directed at adult members of the family group that do not have cubs of their own. Perhaps the aim here is to ensure that the mother and her litter will not have to share food with more adult foxes than necessary.

But in spite of such conflicts, adult vixens sometimes live together in a family group throughout the breeding season. They are often each other's mothers, daughters, or sisters. Kinship goes some way toward explaining why they tolerate each other after all. Natural selection molds animals to behave in ways that ensure their own genes will be passed on, and individuals that are closely related share many of the same genes. For the "helpers"—the subordinate vixens—assisting their mother or sister to reproduce can be a fairly effective way of passing on their own genes. But scientists are not quite sure how useful these helpers actually are, since, of course, they also consume some of the local food resources. Perhaps the helpfulness goes just as much in the other direction—by tolerating the presence of an adult daughter or sister in the home range and thereby giving her a safe place to live, the dominant vixen may also increase the likelihood that her relative will have a chance to reproduce at some point in the future.

I LEFT THE DEN ALONE for a few days before visiting it again. This time, four of the cubs were sitting on the rocky knoll by the entrance to the den when I rounded the bend. They simply stayed sitting where they were and looked at me. The only thing I could think of doing was to sit down on the path too, and once more, I was struck by how much the cubs differed in size. The largest one, which also had redder fur, vanished into the den after a few minutes, accompanied by one of its littermates. The other two remained and sat there looking at me, but my spot in the middle of the path didn't feel like a good place to stay, so I soon got up slowly and walked in a wide arc around the knoll on which the two fox cubs sat. Their eyes followed me as I climbed up the slope to the place where I'd sat on my previous visit. Then they followed. The largest of the two climbed past me to observe me from above. The smallest one came all the way over to me and attacked the backpack I'd thrown down into the heather; it bit and hauled and tugged on the green strap until it got bored and wandered back down to the entrance of the den again.

The two little ones paid no more attention to me but remained aboveground. Sometimes they played, and sometimes they dozed off, snuggled close together. One of them messed around with a big stick, which it managed to drag along with considerable effort. When one of the cubs disappeared into the den, the other was left alone in the open. It lay down to sleep up on the knoll, assuming the same pretzel shape Topsy makes in her basket at home, with the tip of its tail hidden in the base of its throat and its snout tucked beneath its tail; as I sat studying the resting cub through my binoculars, I got the feeling that there must be an adult fox somewhere behind me. It was the sound of birds that alerted me. Woodpeckers and great tits sounded the alarm from the trees higher up, along the top of the little ridge or behind it; these warning sounds were moving in exactly the way they do when birds hop from branch to branch to keep track of a fox that is sneaking around too close to their nesting place. I turned around a few times but saw nothing. When an adult fox actually did turn up, it came from the opposite side of the clearing. It was the yellowish vixen, and one of the cubs came dashing up to it. They greeted each other behind some spruce trees, so I couldn't see whether the cub that had waited aboveground was rewarded for its patience with a snack. At any rate, the two foxes moved up the rock, where they continued to greet each other—tail lashing from side to side, the little cub ran between the legs of the larger fox, and it constantly went over and touched the mouth of the adult fox. The mouth is a sensitive area for dogs and foxes. At home, I notice how difficult Topsy finds it not to lick people's mouths in her enthusiasm, even though she knows we won't let her.

Just as one of the smallest cubs in the litter was enjoying some quality time with a mother or aunt, a terrible scream tore through the forest. The two foxes jumped, then stood slightly apart, ears pricked up. The noise was sharp and grating, somewhere between a short scream and a prolonged bark, and it was repeated at two- or three-second intervals. Only after several such screams did the fox cub decide to go underground. The adult stayed a while longer before slinking off pretty calmly. Perhaps they were used to living with a family member who had a low threshold for sounding the alarm. The screams continued even after the clearing was empty. I was left sitting there, feeling exposed, as the alarm went on and on, and although it was undoubtedly time to leave, my gear was scattered across the forest floor; I thought it would be better to wait until the forest was quiet again before getting up and starting to rummage around.

The screams moved. They completed a full circle around the den and me, without the suspicious fox ever coming into sight. Through the trees, I heard the day's first hikers on the main trail loudly discussing what the strange sounds could be. Oh, it's just me out here bothering the beasts of the forest, I thought. Nothing to make a fuss about; it's just a man in camo gear who's been caught snooping around where the little ones play. I'd promised Helen I would do everything I could not to scare the foxes she'd shown me. Now I felt as if I'd let her down badly. The hikers trudged onward and vanished, and down by the entrance to the den, among the tree roots at the bottom of the hill, I saw a fox cub peek out. It jumped every time there was another scream. When I leaned forward to get a better look, it disappeared into the den again. The screams had circled me and the den for the second time when I got it into my head that I wanted to see this suspicious fox. The situation was becoming untenable, but in a way it felt more drastic to start rummaging around with my baggage than to creep carefully up to the top of the hill and peer over the edge. There, just across a dip in the landscape, sat a copper-red fox, screaming in the same steady rhythm as before. It looked me straight in the eyes. I turned and started to pack my bag, and as I worked, some crows came along and made even more of a racket around the screaming vixen. I saw her again as I trudged away from the scene. The crows hung in the air above her. She screamed and screamed, and not until I was well over the next hillock did the forest fall silent again.

IT FELT AS IF it was about time to leave the foxes in peace. Far too many people were tramping across their den as it was, and it probably would have been better for me to stay at home, but I couldn't quite stop. My fox-watching had developed into a kind of obsession.

Sleep deprivation wasn't exactly helping my mental balance. The plan I hatched out that very evening before falling into a deep sleep was this: I set my alarm clock as absurdly early as last time so that I'd have time to brew a thermos of coffee and make a snack while I was waking up. In my backpack, I placed two wildlife cameras. I got up as planned, got in my car, drove an hour to the parking lot on the edge of the wood, and marched to the den. Everything was quiet there. I set up the two wildlife cameras and left them standing there as silent witnesses while I took a long hike in the morning sun.

YOU'RE NOT REALLY supposed to set up wildlife cameras in places where people go hiking. I hadn't gotten permission from the landowner either, so this was a bit out of line. But, as I argued to myself, there was little chance anyone would come by this particular place so early on a weekday morning. Just as the first hikers started to appear on the busier main trail, I returned and hastily took down the cameras. And what did I get to see? There were no people in the recordings. Nor did the cubs show themselves, only adult foxes that stopped by for a quick inspection. I'm guessing they'd had enough of people and had moved the cubs elsewhere during the night. Sooner or later, a fox family tends to establish a new base away from the den. In this case, they probably decided to do it sooner rather than later, and I like to think that the hikers and orienteers contributed to that decision, along with my own fox-watching.

Perhaps the nervous copper-red vixen had made the move without alerting the cubs' father. At any rate, the first fox to show up in front of the camera was an adult male. He came bearing a triangular slice of pizza for the cubs, and since he'd started shedding his winter coat later than the two vixens, he looked like a real ragamuffin. The fox father stopped abruptly, with the pizza slice in his mouth, when he became aware of the wildlife camera. He laid back his ears, stared, and sniffed before vanishing out of the shot. Four minutes later, he returned without the pizza slice to take a closer look. He scented the air in the direction of the camera, sniffed on the ground where the cubs used to play, and slunk off. A roe deer peered into the clearing, as well as a couple of thrushes. The copper-red fox, the one that had screamed so hideously twenty-four hours before, came by for an inspection, maybe to confirm that the place was clear of cubs. She did a large circuit of the clearing and the surrounding forest, stuck her snout into the den entrance between the tree roots, then vanished into the forest again. My last sighting of the foxes from the den beside the forest trail was the straw-yellow vixen passing by on the outer edge of the frame. She was carrying something in her jaws that I assumed must have been a snack for the cubs.

MY TAKEAWAY FROM all of this was that you mustn't spend too long sitting by a fox's den. After a brief spell watching fox cubs, it's time to head off, because adult foxes are wary around the den. Anyone wanting to achieve the difficult feat of observing their interactions with the cubs must have a plan. Some suggest setting up a seat or other observation platform in a tree. The observer's scent would be carried off more easily by the wind—and foxes don't pay as much attention to what's going on far above. Another lesson I've learned is not to set up wildlife cameras so near an active fox's den again either. The suspicious gaze of the father fox with the pizza slice was enough to convince me of that.

Urban Foxes

SOME WEEKS LATER, I see a video clip of a young fox trying to get into a house. It was recorded in the area of Oslo where the city meets the forest, not so far from the fox's den beside the trail and orienteering checkpoint. Of course, I don't know whether the cub is one of those I've seen before, but it isn't unlikely. "This one is too tame," writes the woman who filmed the young fox. Based on the comments below her post, it seems several other people in the neighborhood have had visits too.

The video can be seen in a Facebook group where Oslo's Agency for Urban Environment invites the city's inhabitants to share their encounters with wildlife. The agency staff play down the drama in their responses to people who have seen foxes: There aren't all that many foxes in Oslo. They aren't dangerous. You should be glad of the chance to see one, and it's hardly unusual for the cubs to be hungry, curious, and trusting. Nonetheless, the agency constantly repeats the plea: don't feed the foxes in your garden. In neighborhoods where some inhabitants leave food out, they often end up in conflict with neighbors who aren't as keen on pushy foxes.

This year, the island of Malmøya is where the urban foxes are really causing a stir. My home looks straight across the fjord to the green island, with its little nature reserve, houses set in gardens, and foxes that are almost unbelievably tame compared with the ones that slink around my own neighborhood— just a few miles away as the crow flies. On our side of the fjord, the foxes raid henhouses under cover of darkness, but we seldom catch a glimpse of them. On the other side, by contrast, they pay people visits. "Had to chuck 'Mikkel Rev' out of bed," reads the headline of a news report from the area. One photo taken by a resident shows a sopping wet, adult fox standing on the veranda in broad daylight, staring in through the window. The fox cubs jump on trampolines. They chew a wicker basket to pieces on the lawn. Some inhabitants have had regular visits from foxes for years and are fond of them, while others have had enough of foxy pranks. People who use the marina on one of the neighboring islands complain about unwanted visits in their boats—"I screamed when I woke and found it beside me" runs one newspaper headline. Just inland, a dog owner reports that their dog was injured in a fight with foxes. "The foxes are pushy because they get fed," Tea Turtumøygard of the Agency for Urban Environment tells a local

A red fox peers in through the window.
Malmøya Island, Oslo, Norway.

PHOTO: MORTEN LUNDE

newspaper. "If people stop feeding them, the foxes will go away."

Of course, when you've struggled to catch even a glimpse of a fox, the idea of foxes on trampolines sounds irresistible. One bright summer evening, I make the trip to Malmøya and spy an adult fox stealing along the narrow main road that runs the length of the island—with something flat, round, and white in its mouth. It looks like a paper plate. The road is so narrow here, with walls, fences, and hedges on either side, that oncoming cars almost have to squeeze past pedestrians like the fox and me. A massive SUV stops so that the driver can point a cell phone out of the window and film the fox from above as they pass one another. The fox heads off into a stand of trees. Annoyingly enough, that is all I get to see, because most of the excitement here goes on in private gardens, and you can't just gate-crash.

A few weeks later, I'm reminded of the foxes of Malmøya when an acquaintance forwards a video he was sent by a colleague who went out there for a swim. "I don't have any food," says the friendly voice behind the camera. But her tone changes when the fox grabs her beach bag in its mouth and runs off with it. I jump into my car that same afternoon and take another drive around the fjord to Malmøya, but there are no foxes to be seen along the beaches; this time I only get to *hear* the fox, up in a garden I can't enter. Something is clearly making it uneasy. The urban fox on Malmøya screams just like the suspicious vixen by the den in the forest.

THE PHENOMENON OF urban foxes is by no means exclusive to Oslo. The red fox has gradually taken over many European cities, and the United Kingdom in particular is famed for its large urban fox population. One of the reasons for this may be that the British Isles have long been free of both rabies and fox tapeworm, which probably makes the fox a more welcome garden guest than in many places in mainland Europe. In Bristol, southwest England, urban foxes have been the subjects of a long-term research program. Some districts of the city have extremely dense fox populations, which often eat, play, and breed in people's gardens, but this population was nearly wiped out by a local mange epidemic in 1994. Much like in Scandinavia some years earlier, researchers used the outbreak as an opportunity to conduct a natural experiment. They found out a great deal about how flexible foxes' social lives are by comparing the situation before the arrival of mange and just after, when there was suddenly much more space.

Given how class-conscious the British are, they have of course also pondered where the urban fox fits into the social hierarchy. In their 2001 book, *Urban Foxes*, zoologists Stephen Harris and Phil Baker of the University of Bristol concluded that urban foxes are middle-class. Their point was that the places with the most foxes tended to be the extensive neighborhoods of semidetached houses with relatively large gardens that were built on the outskirts of many English cities in the interwar period. In these districts, with their relatively prosperous inhabitants, the gardens were big enough to contain small bushes and hedges that provided hiding places, or an outbuilding beneath which the fox could dig a den. In many cities, the red fox began to establish itself in these sorts of neighborhoods during the postwar years, and later spread to the inner cities, industrial zones, and residential areas that are less ideally designed, from a fox's point of view.

Stephen Harris, the grand old man of urban fox research, is also an eager advocate for these animals. They are not starving, he tends to explain, and they are no more diseased than foxes in the countryside. Sometimes people think they look mangy when they are simply molting. I am less certain whether readers' fears will be allayed by his assurance that domestic animals form only "a very small part of the diet" of the urban fox, but, as Harris also points out, people who leave rabbits or chickens outdoors at night should secure their cages against predators regardless of whether there are few or many foxes in the neighborhood. The risk of your cat being killed by a fox is vanishingly small compared with the risk of its dying in a traffic accident, even in neighborhoods that are crammed full of foxes. Cats and foxes tend to sidestep each other. Yet even the friends of urban foxes concede that foxes can be a nuisance for garden owners—digging up flower beds, say; excreting on the lawn; running off with objects; or chewing shoes to bits.

The foxes of Bristol get a large share of their diet from the food people give them. *Urban Foxes* warmly recommends feeding foxes, not because they need it but because people get so much pleasure from observing foxes close-up. In a TV documentary from 2017, Stephen Harris and his wife show how they themselves leave food on the lawn, so that they can watch the foxes through their living room window. Bristol's local authorities, however, advise against feeding; still, like their counterparts in Oslo, they downplay the situation, emphasizing that the risk of foxes harming people or cats is low. Over the years, there have been a few cases of foxes biting and injuring people in the United Kingdom, including newborn babies or small children left alone in the garden—or even indoors with doors or windows open. While scary, these are extremely rare events. The risk of being bitten by a dog is much higher for both adults and children. There are no known cases of Britons dying from a fox bite— the country has, after all, been rabies-free for a long time—whereas people there are regularly killed by dogs. As Stephen Harris says, it is undoubtedly a bad idea to get foxes used to being hand-fed, or to invite them into one's home.

IN URBAN SETTINGS, shooting foxes or otherwise controlling their population is particularly difficult. It would be hard to get rid of urbanized foxes altogether, even if one wished to. There are so many different kinds of fox food in large towns and cities—rats and mice, ducks and pigeons, earthworms in the parks, and (of course) food waste from households, eateries, and people eating on the go. That is why you can see red foxes all over Oslo, even in the very center. In practice, the question is how we want to coexist with urban foxes and, in particular, whether we want to encourage them to become numerous in residential areas and confident around people. The problem with feeding foxes is that the consequences extend far beyond one's own garden. That's especially true in densely populated areas. If I lived in a really remote spot, I wouldn't hesitate to leave out snacks for the foxes so that I could watch them. As it is, I don't.

Farmed Foxes

THE FOX IS ALSO a domestic animal and has been for more than a century. During the peak years of the fox farming industry, there were, in fact, several times more caged foxes than wild foxes in Norway. However, after much fuss, the Norwegian government passed a bill shutting down all fur farms by 2025. One of the issues debated in the run-up to the bill's passage was the nature of farmed foxes: Were they domestic animals deep down, adapted to life in captivity? Or were they still like the foxes out in the forests and in the mountains—had they retained so much of the wild animal that they suffered in the tedium of their cramped cages?

PRINCE EDWARD ISLAND in Atlantic Canada is the place where foxes were outfoxed by humans once and for all, and became the progenitors of millions of descendants in captivity. As early as 1880, the first silver foxes—red foxes with black and silver-gray coats—were trapped there and kept for breeding purposes. Their pelts were highly sought-after, and silver fox breeding proved profitable. Among fox breeders, the term "silver fox" confusingly acquired two separate meanings. The first referred to the fox variety with black and silver fur. The second referred to any animal of the red fox species, *Vulpes vulpes*, that was kept for fur farming—including those with fur in colors other than black and silver. Over the years, breeders crossed foxes with reddish fur with animals from the established strain of captive silver foxes to produce new varieties, with color descriptions such as red fox and gold fox. These also came to be referred to as silver fox varieties.

Just prior to the First World War, a Norwegian businessman decided to take a big gamble on silver foxes. Wholesaler Arne Christensen bought a single pair from a Canadian breeder for $10,000—a staggering sum at the time, equivalent to roughly $200,000 in today's money. The silver fox pair, Amund and Amanda, arrived in Kristiania (modern-day Oslo) on a boat from America on January 1, 1914, accompanied by a Canadian lawyer who traveled at Christensen's expense. Amund and Amanda were the very first members of the European silver fox population.

Many people were keen to try their hand at fur production, and in the early years, Christensen earned good money from selling parent animals to other breeders. More livestock was also imported from Canada. A new color variety known as platinum fox, where the animals had paler fur with silver-gray and white markings, achieved record prices. The first platinum fox to be found and intentionally bred was a male cub called Mons, which was born into an otherwise normally colored silver fox litter at a fur farm in northern Norway. Mons had thousands of platinum fox descendants.

THE ARCTIC FOX gave rise to a separate line of farmed foxes. Wild Arctic foxes were captured in many places—in North America, on Greenland, Iceland, and Svalbard—and used for breeding purposes. The blue fox color variety, one of the two that occur in the wild, was the most highly sought-after. That is why "blue fox" has become the collective term applied to Arctic foxes kept for breeding, regardless of their actual color. Fashion goes in waves as we know, so over the years, blue fox varieties have sometimes been more popular than silver fox varieties and vice versa—and the dominant species in the fur farms has fluctuated accordingly. Farmers have also crossbred the two fox species. Red foxes and Arctic foxes don't usually mate successfully in the wild, but hybrids became easier to produce in the 1980s, when farmers adopted artificial insemination. Experiments with such hybrids were part of the constant efforts to develop new and unique fur varieties that could command particularly high prices.

FUR IS AN exclusive material, a luxury product, which is why the fur-farming industry has been sensitive to shifts in demand. For a long time, government authorities did their best to help, because this was the kind of business politicians found easy to love—it created jobs in rural areas, it could be highly profitable, and it generated tax revenues. Fur production even had a glamorous sheen to it, since it provided royalty, film stars, and other celebrities with spectacular garments.

Around the turn of the millennium, though, attitudes started to change. A warning shot across the bows came in Norway in 1994, when an ethics committee set up by the Ministry of Agriculture and Food recommended dismantling the entire fur-farming industry. It took the view that the carnivorans kept in fur farms—foxes and minks—were fairly similar to their wild forebears and had "a fundamental need to form part of social groups, claim territory, roam, hunt, gather food supplies, build dens, etc." It was unfeasible to give them all this in a profitable fur-farming business. Supporters of the fur-farming industry claimed that many parts of the fox's behavioral repertoire became less relevant once humans ensured that they were kept well fed and watered at all times, protected from enemies, and equipped with wooden den crates in which to give birth to their cubs. They thought foxes were unlikely to miss working for their food and struggling for survival.

The Council for Animal Ethics' report was roundly rejected by the Norwegian authorities. In Sweden, on the other hand, a similar assessment led to rules that made fur farming impossible, practically speaking. In 1995, the Swedish authorities approved a bill stipulating that foxes should be allowed room for activity, including a requirement that they must have opportunities to dig. That was easier said than done. Even in its infancy, the fur-farming industry had found that parasites such as intestinal worms spread rapidly among foxes that lived in close quarters in enclosures with soil or sand floors. The wire mesh floors of modern fur farms are the only practical solution the industry has come up with to ensure adequate hygiene when large numbers of foxes are kept in a restricted space.

In Norway, the authorities focused on making fox farming more animal-friendly, through reforms that were possible for the industry to implement in practical terms. The animals were to be handled more humanely, for example. Breeders had previously used neck tongs, which enabled them to work with scared or aggressive foxes without getting bitten. From 1998, the use of these tongs was restricted—they could only be used in special circumstances, such as when the fox was being put down or artificially inseminated. Instead, breeders were supposed to try to make fur animals tamer by selecting calm and trusting animals for breeding—so that the resulting foxes would be better adapted to life in captivity. This measure took some time to implement; interest varied from farm to farm, and the breeding of fur animals was managed locally by each individual breeder.

OVER THE NEW MILLENNIUM, political support for fox farming started to diminish and Norway eventually joined the many European countries that had already banned keeping foxes in fur farms, including Sweden, Denmark, Austria, Italy, the Netherlands, and the United Kingdom. The Norwegian Parliament agreed that the industry would be granted a transition period lasting until February 1, 2025. For now, Finland remains a major producer of fox fur—they produced about 700,000 fox pelts in 2022—but even there the industry's future is contested. There is also fur farming in countries such as China and Russia, and a few fox farms are still operating in Canada and the United States.

IN MID-JULY, I got in my car and drove to the Hemsedal valley to visit a Norwegian fur farm before it was too late. Once there, I watched as fur farmer Sigbjørn Kirkebøen lifted a metal grating hatch, then bent from the waist into one of the cages so he could reach the cubs that were pressed against the rear wall. He picked one up in his fist, then held it close to his body as he bent down to fish out another. As soon as they were out of the cage, the coal-black cubs with white-tipped tails stopped wriggling; the little foxes, aged around seven weeks, simply hung there in the fur farmer's hands and gazed wide-eyed at their surroundings, including me, as their mother observed the scene from her vantage point on a wire mesh shelf, high up in the cage she shared with her litter. We were standing in a long wooden building with a pitched, corrugated iron roof and a row of fox cages lining either side of the central passage. It was breezy in there. Daylight and wind entered the wire mesh cages from the side.

The fur farm consisted of eight such buildings, which stood parallel to one another on a plain near the river. We went over to the next longhouse, which contained cubs that had been born a bit earlier in the spring and had already been separated from their mother. Again, the farmer took out two small foxes from a litter of six. He brought them outside so I could take photos of them in better light.

"Look here. They're starting to grow silver hair," Kirkebøen said.

And he was quite right—these silver fox cubs, which were probably nine weeks old, had started to live up to their name. Over the underlying black color, pale tips of hair were visible, creating the silvery shimmer that made their fur so sought-after. In six months' time, these little foxes would be fully grown; over the fall, their winter coat would grow dense and glossy— and just before Christmas, the animals would be put down and skinned so that their fur could become raw material for coats and other garments, unless they were selected as breeding animals, in which case they would last a few more seasons.

Kirkebøen's farm reflected the regulations the Norwegian authorities had brought in to improve fur animals' living conditions over the past few decades. In each cage, there were wooden sticks that were more or less gnawed to pieces. These sticks were so-called activity objects, intended to give cubs and adult foxes something to do in the otherwise dull environment of the cage. The adult foxes also had a bone to gnaw on. The wire mesh shelves beneath the ceiling of the cage, which gave the foxes a lookout spot they seemed to appreciate, was another measure intended to improve their well-being. In addition, new regulations had come in regarding cage size. For example, a vixen with large cubs, like the first ones we met, was required to have a floor space of 2.0 square meters (roughly seven square feet), although in practice, they often had 2.4 square meters (about eight square feet) at their disposal. Half of that area was the minimum requirement for two independent cubs during the period leading up to December, when they would be put down and skinned. Most of the cages were divided into sections, with hatches between them that could be opened or closed. This meant that several foxes could share the entire area, or could be separated if necessary. According to regulations, the growing cubs should be allowed to spend time with one or more of their siblings, so that they could socialize and engage in the play-fighting typical of young foxes—as long as it didn't get too aggressive.

We came to a building that housed adult silver foxes, one per cage. Without any particular fuss, Kirkebøen performed what was clearly his party trick. He leaned into the cage of a solitary adult vixen, who was lying on a shelf. With one hand, he took hold of her hind legs and pulled her hindquarters toward him; then, placing his other hand beneath her chest for support, he lifted the large vixen out of the cage and held her close to his own body. She regarded me with a seemingly skeptical look on her vulpine face, but she was quite calm and gave no sign of wanting to wriggle away or bite either me or the unprotected hands of the fox farmer.

"Twenty years ago, we didn't have animals we could handle like this," he said.

Some foxes could be tamer than others in those days too, but now most foxes on the farm were so tame that Kirkebøen could lift them up with his bare hands without worrying. He had been early to embark on systematic breeding to produce tamer foxes. Indeed, his breeding work was the reason I knew about him and his silver foxes at all—the first time I saw them was in an informational film for fur farmers produced by the Norwegian University of Life Sciences (NMBU), with funding from the Norwegian Fur Farming Association.

The film was about how to breed more trusting silver foxes. It showed one fox that barked at a gloved hand and another that climbed up the cage wall to escape. These kinds of animals should not be used for breeding. The hand test—which simply involved sticking a hand into the cage and trying to touch the fox—was one of the methods the university researchers recommended for selecting breeding animals. It was best to use the foxes that didn't merely tolerate the hand and give it a bit of a sniff, but which also allowed themselves to be touched without shying away—for example, animals that allowed their fur to be stroked or their neck to be scratched.

After just five or six years of breeding, Kirkebøen was producing tamer animals. That made everyday life on the farm easier and more enjoyable, the film explained. The aim of the breeding efforts was to produce a line of foxes that would be genetically predisposed to be trustful. It was also important to teach each individual fox to trust people by, for example, handing out snacks as rewards after handling the animal. At the time the film was produced, the future of the industry was the subject of heated debate, but fur farmers were still looking ahead back then.

PERSONALLY, I DIDN'T KNOW anyone who wore fur. In my childhood, fur coats were largely the preserve of old ladies, and fur had recently gained such a bad reputation that people avoided using garments they already had in their wardrobes because fur was associated with cruelty to animals. International campaigns in which supermodels swore they would rather go naked than wear fur probably helped. In countries around the world, animal welfare activists protested against fur farming with attention-grabbing break-ins and sabotage actions. Minks and foxes were released from their cages. Fur businesses were vandalized. Facilities producing fur animal feed were even fire-bombed, and fur animal researchers at the Norwegian University of Life Sciences also had their facilities destroyed at one point.

While these actions were, of course, both frightening and costly for those affected, they barely contributed to the political victory of the opponents of fur. Another form of activism probably proved more effective—activists got inside fur farms, first by climbing over fences at nighttime to film, later by going undercover with hidden cameras in collaboration with a documentary film producer. The result was that the industry's defenders constantly found themselves having to comment on photos and video clips of fur farms that were most definitely failing to follow regulations—there were images of minks and foxes with sores and bitten-off tails, of rundown facilities and poor cleanliness, and of fur farmers talking about how they went about making a good impression on the state inspectors without having to follow the rules. People in the industry protested about the impression the TV reports created. They said that the images showed exceptions rather than the typical situation. They distanced themselves from the violations of rules and expelled individual members of the Norwegian Fur Farming Association. But the damage was done. TV documentaries and news bulletins showing examples of terrible animal welfare helped bring the industry into disrepute, and undoubtedly weakened political support for fur farming.

"It hasn't been easy," Sigbjørn Kirkebøen said as we stood outside the fox houses in the pale light of an overcast day. "We've faced very aggressive opposition. We've been kept on the back foot all the way, and with hindsight I must admit we've been far too defensive and cautious about showing off the industry—we've almost lived in hiding."

From inside the nearest building came agitated animal voices. The soundscape created by the foxes was more reminiscent of a tropical rainforest than anything you'd expect to hear in Hemsedal, and it distracted me slightly from the conversation.

When the future of fur farming was still up for debate, Kirkebøen used to show groups of visitors around the farm in an attempt to present the industry in a better light. He and his colleagues often pointed out that their most dogged opponents weren't just against fur farming, but other livestock farming too. If they could get fur farms shut down, they would go after meat, milk, and egg production next. The way Kirkebøen saw it, those leading the opposition represented values that the majority of Norwegians didn't share; they might, for example, think that individuals of other species had the same worth and deserved as much protection as human beings.

But, I asked, surely veterinarians posed the biggest problem for fur farmers during the debate, didn't they? Both the Norwegian Veterinary Association and the government-run Norwegian Veterinarian Institute had spoken in favor of shutting down the fur-farming industry, and you could hardly call them extremist activists. On the other hand, the livestock scientists at the Norwegian University of Life Sciences, which had been studying fur animals' behavior and measures to improve well-being in the cages since the 1980s, had judged the welfare of the farm foxes to be "adequate," as long as farmers followed regulations.

Kirkebøen shook his head slightly when I mentioned the veterinarians. There was little resistance among those who had proper expertise in the area of fur farming, he said. But few veterinarians had practical experience of fur animals. His impression was that increasing numbers of veterinarians were working solely with pets, and that resulted in less knowledge about livestock in general.

I didn't know what to say to that. I knew nothing of the internal workings of the veterinary profession. But when it came to the attitudes of people in general, Kirkebøen undoubtedly had a point. Our experience with pets has considerable bearing on our views about animal welfare. If you think of the fox as an animal that resembles your own dog or cat, it probably feels wrong for it to have to spend its entire life in a cage whose longest side is equivalent to one or two body lengths, tail included. Things might seem different if you viewed the silver fox as livestock, like the cow, say. Most people have no qualms about drinking milk that is produced by separating the calf from its mother one to three days after birth, even though no one has claimed that cows lack maternal instinct or that calves prefer to be on their own.

YET THE ARGUMENT for shutting down the fur-farming industry was not that fur animals resembled pets, but rather that they resembled their wild relatives. Silver foxes, blue foxes, and minks were "barely domesti-cated," and therefore ill-suited to life in captivity, according to the Norwegian Veterinary Association and animal welfare organizations.

So how different are the silver foxes at fur farms to wild red foxes? Of course, farmed foxes are influenced by the fact that they grew up in a different environ-ment. Beyond that, domestication has shaped them to a certain extent—that is to say, their genetic makeup is somewhat adapted to life in captivity, although they have had much less time to adapt than, say, chickens, cows, or pigs, which have been domestic animals for millennia. Domestication is a process that begins as soon as animals start to live in captivity or in close contact with people. A kind of sifting-out happens at that point, even in the absence of intentional breeding efforts. The animals that react most strongly to stimuli—such as foxes that panic every time a human approaches, or are constantly enraged by the fox in the adjoining cage—may simply find it difficult to survive and reproduce. The ones that resign themselves to their situation and settle down cope better because in captivity, as elsewhere, the best adapted individuals are the ones that succeed. Focused breeding aimed at producing more trusting animals, the kind Sigbjørn Kirkebøen has engaged in, speeds up the process of domestication.

Of course, research alone cannot tell us whether living in a cage is good enough for foxes. The cage environment is undoubtedly dull, and provides little room for activity. Behavioral scientists who have worked with silver foxes in the fur-farming industry say that the animals appear to have retained the entire behavioral repertoire of their wild forebears. The difference is that they are less "reactive," meaning that it either takes more to make them react or they don't react as strongly. In other words, it isn't as easy for farmed foxes to get as carried away, excited, or scared as their wild counterparts. This calmer temperament is among the hallmarks of domesticated animals, but domestication is a question of degree, not either-or.

Silver foxes from fur farms have, in fact, been the object of the largest and longest scientific experiment ever conducted to map what happens when animals are domesticated. The experiment, which started in the Soviet Union in the 1950s and continues in Russia to this day, directly inspired Norwegian breeders' efforts to obtain more trusting animals in fur farms. But the more than seventy-year-old history of the domestication experiment has wider implications than that. Russian silver fox research has also provided new answers to the questions of how dogs became tame, how suitable the fox is as a pet, and even how humans once learned to tame their own wildness.

Pet Foxes

IT ISN'T JUST the flesh-and-blood fox that is a versatile creature. In literature too, we meet the most diverse fox characters, which are sometimes cast in an entirely different mold than the rascally Mikkel Rev and Reynard the Fox. In the French children's classic *The Little Prince*, for example, the prince meets a fox that turns out to be a wise and sensitive being, with greater self-insight than many humans. "My life is monotonous," says the fox. "I hunt chickens; people hunt me. All chickens are just alike, and all men are just alike. So I'm rather bored. But if you tame me, my life will be filled with sunshine. I'll know the sound of footsteps that will be different from all the rest. Other footsteps send me back underground. Yours will call me out of my burrow like music." The little prince never gets time to tame the fox. Yet he gains something from the meeting because it reminds him about the value of friendship, of love, and of the kind of lasting relationships with others that the prince himself already has, but which he has left behind. This reminder makes him yearn for home.

It seems unlikely that real wild animals long to be tamed. For us humans, though, the desire to adopt animals is so deep-rooted that people have tried to tame red foxes over and over and over again. I've come across plenty of such stories. One friend sent me a black-and-white photo of his uncle who kept a red fox in the 1970s. The fox was as cuddly and tame as a dog, the uncle claimed in an old newspaper clipping, and used to join him when he performed as a magician. A few years back, a copper-red pet fox whose owner had bought it from a fur farm as a cub won Instagram fame as Ayla the Fox—until it escaped and died. In my own neck of the woods, I met a man who told me he had once taken care of a wild fox cub after its mother died. The family cats helped house-train the fox, he claimed. But after a while, they had to shut the cat-flap and check the young fox's mouth every time it went out, because it liked to steal all kinds of things from the house and hide them outdoors. Another guy I met used to feed a fox that came to visit him. The two of them became closer and closer, and when his furry friend caught mange, the man tricked both the veterinarian and the pharmacist into ordering prescription medicine for a fictitious dog called Mikkel.

In other words, the fox can be tamed in a way. The great Russian fox experiment made this easier than ever before, by breeding foxes that had an innate talent for socializing with humans, not unlike what we see with dogs. So the story starts in the Soviet Union, where fur farming was built up into a major industry from the interwar years onward. After the Second World War, fur exports brought in much-needed foreign currency revenue.

In the 1950s, a Russian biologist called Dmitry Belyaev (1917–1985) found that the fur-farming business lent itself perfectly to a large-scale experiment he was keen to conduct. Silver foxes made for suitable experimental animals, and fur production also provided useful cover, because Belyaev could pretend that the sole purpose of his research was to make the foxes easier to handle so that fur production would become more efficient. What really interested him, though, was fundamental biological research of the sort that met with skepticism from the Soviet authorities. Belyaev was interested in genetics and evolution, but well into the postwar period, the authorities continued to espouse an alternative view of the relationship between evolution, nature, and nurture—dismissing concepts such as genes and genetic material as "bourgeois science."

Belyaev wanted to study how wild animals had once become domestic animals, and, in particular, how wolves became dogs. So he wished to recreate the domestication process and study how it worked. His experiment started with silver foxes from the Soviet fur farms. These were not exactly wild animals, but they didn't like people. If the animal technicians stuck a hand in the cage, the foxes would often bite, so the technicians had to use thick, protective gloves.

The foxes in the experiment were kept in cages much like those at the fur farms, but in a special research facility in Siberia. As they grew, the foxes received carefully allotted doses of human contact, in the form of repeated tests that aimed to show whether or not the fox tolerated and, potentially, sought out contact with people. The technicians held out a hand, offered food, and tried to pet and handle the cubs. The ones that bit or ran away failed the test. The ones that were most trusting and keen on contact were selected for breeding. Thus, the experiment continued through generation after generation of foxes, year after year, decade after decade. When Belyaev died, others took over. The result was that the scientists obtained a population of foxes that didn't merely tolerate contact, but actively sought out humans, even when no food was being offered. The foxes that were bred for tameness wagged their tails, whined, sniffed, and licked when they were given the opportunity to meet people; put simply, they behaved like friendly dogs.

The experiment, which has continued to this day, shows that foxes' attitudes to humans, whether they enjoy or fear contact with people, partly stem from innate and inherited traits. In other words, it's in their genes. The environment they grow up in has an impact too—even foxes that have been bred for tameness have to get used to humans during their cubhood, and only when they are taken out of their cage environment and kept as a kind of pet is their potential for forming bonds with humans fully realized. On the other hand, many foxes that are not specially bred for tameness can still become trusting if they have very close contact with humans as cubs. It is just much easier to gain the trust of the foxes from the Belyaev experiment.

The aim of this experiment was not just to find out whether tameness was hereditary. Belyaev also wanted to investigate an observation that Charles Darwin had once made. Darwin pointed out that domesticated animals shared some visible traits. As well as being more sociable toward people, domesticated animals were physically distinct from their wild counterparts—yet it was hard to see the purpose of these changes. For example, domestic animals often had more variable color markings, in many cases including patterns of light and dark patches on their bodies; and some had drooping ears, even though they were descended from wild forebears whose ears stood straight up. Some people have since referred to the suite of traits shared by different domesticated species as the "domestication syndrome"—although this is a somewhat controversial term; far from all domestic animals show all the traits usually associated with the syndrome. Experts in the field still debate how many similarities there really are between the ways different animal species change as a result of domestication, as well as the conclusions that can be drawn from the great fox experiment.

Belyaev thought some of the visible differences between wild and tame animals were simply side effects of changes in the animals' temperament. When people selected an animal that was calm, friendly, and unafraid—and therefore suited to a life in proximity to humans—what they obtained, in practice, was an animal with slightly different genes and slightly different hormone production, which affected both the animal's behavior and its physical development from the fetal stage onward.

The Russian researchers who continued the domestication project after Belyaev's death claim that the experiment has recreated the domestication syndrome in foxes. Some of the foxes bred for tameness—admittedly only a small minority—display doglike physical changes, such as slightly drooping ears, a curl in the tail, and white markings, including a variant with a blaze (a white patch on the forehead). They report changes in the foxes' skull shape, which are reminiscent of the differences between dogs and wolves. In addition, they have seen signs of an extended mating season. This last point is a matter of interest because one of the most striking biological differences between dogs and wolves is that dogs' fertility is not restricted to a brief annual mating period.

Belyaev suggested an explanation for the domestication syndrome that others have also touched upon—that domesticated animals acquire a kind of developmental disorder whereby they retain childish traits as adults. That might explain their greater trustfulness and sociability, and may at least be consistent with some of the physical changes observed in domesticated animals such as dogs. A newer and more precise theory that attempts to explain the domestication syndrome is that a change in the growth of certain cells, known as neural crest cells, occurs early in fetal development. These cells generate tissue in many places in the body and may be associated with changes in both the nervous system and visible features, such as ear shape or white patches on the coat.

The debate over the domestication syndrome is fascinating because animal husbandry is such an important part of human history. Many of us have a close relationship with dogs and cats in particular and are keen for information about how wild beasts were able to become cuddly companions. But there is also another reason why the domestication syndrome sparks so much interest: humanity's own evolutionary history reflects similar traits. The hallmark of our species is our unique capacity to trust each other, collaborate with each other, and share the benefits.

This capacity requires us not to be too easily roused to anger toward—or fear of—the people around us. Put simply, we must at some point have domesticated ourselves. The changes in fetal development and hormonal system that made us into more sociable creatures may have resembled the changes that transformed wolves into dogs and made Russian silver foxes fonder of humans.

A scientist with the suitably mammalian name of Brian Hare recently summed up what he calls the human self-domestication hypothesis, building largely on what we know about other species such as dogs, foxes, and apes. Professor Hare starts with dogs. At some point, they domesticated themselves—that is to say, canids began to live in close quarters with people and to feed off their refuse. These dogs had to be fearless enough to approach people and harmless enough for people to accept their presence. The dogs that also succeeded in ingratiating themselves with people by being cute or useful may have had a snack slung their way now and again. In this way, natural selection began to reward sociable and human-friendly dogs long before anyone thought about breeding.

One of the distinguishing traits of dogs is that they are far better than wolves at interpreting human signals, such as pointing. Brian Hare conducted an experiment with the Russian Belyaev foxes and found that they too had a special talent for interpreting people's pointing and gaze. They were better at this than the foxes in the control group—silver foxes from fur farms that had not been systematically selected for tameness. Attentiveness to human body language was not among the selection criteria in the breeding experiment. That arose as a byproduct of a calmer, friendlier, and more trusting disposition. So maybe a similar effect once made it easier for the dog to domesticate itself—if the capacity to understand human signals simply came about as a side effect of a sociable temperament. And perhaps we humans were able to develop our own unique way of communicating among ourselves—language—because we became tamer, more sociable in nature.

Another important trait shared by dogs and Belyaev foxes is that the formative period in which they are open to bonding with humans lasts longer than that of their wild forebears. While it is also possible to tame other fox and wolf cubs, it requires more intensive effort within a shorter window of time. The relatively long period in which puppies and Belyaev foxes are open to being tamed is somewhat reminiscent of humans; after all, we have extremely long childhoods in which we are malleable, quick to learn, and open to impressions.

Hare also considers our closest living relatives among the apes and our even-closer extinct relatives, known to us from archeological finds such as bones and the remains of artifacts they gradually learned to produce. Running through the evolution of the modern human—*Homo sapiens*—Hare sees traces of a kind of domestication process. Humans rewarded each other for friendliness and willingness to cooperate, or punished each other for the opposite. In this way, individuals with a more peaceable disposition were successful and had more descendants.

HUMAN NATURE IS, of course, at least as diverse as that of the fox. One of our odder distinguishing features is our urge to bind so many different species of animals to us. We already have a long list of well-established domestic animals: pigs, cats, silkworms, goldfish, water buffalo, salmon, reindeer, and budgies; in addition, people everywhere have tried to tame wild animals they happen to come across—as illustrated by photos of Indigenous children in the Amazonian rainforest carrying lizards, monkeys, and birds.

Naturally enough, newspaper articles about the Belyaev foxes have made many people wish they had a pet fox. For a few years, these domesticated foxes were even marketed as pets in the United States and Europe—although the reality is that even they are unsuitable for most private individuals. Admittedly, they are easier to tame than other foxes; they are more friendly and affectionate if you bring them up roughly the same way you would a puppy or a kitten. People with experience of keeping foxes as pets say that they have a willful attitude that is more reminiscent of cats than dogs. The problem is that foxes also have frenetic activity levels. Belyaev foxes, like most foxes, are far from placid animals, and their behavior is often unpredictable. One fox owner speaks of the time she put down a cup of coffee only to find that her devoted fox had peed in it while she was looking the other way. Even the Siberian foxes get up to so much mischief that very few people could cope with having them in the house long term. The smell of fox is another reason why pet foxes must generally live in outdoor spaces that are properly secured against digging and climbing, although I dare say you could take them for a walk with collar and leash. In brief, it's inadvisable to keep a fox as a pet.

Pet foxes have been banned in many places across the world, including a number of U.S. states and Canadian provinces. But we can still dream of having a fox in our lives. So let's listen to the fox in *The Little Prince*, as he tells the prince how to go about taming him. "'It would have been better to return at the same time,' the fox said. 'For instance, if you come at four in the afternoon, I'll begin to be happy by three.'" The prince must be very patient. He must keep his distance to start off with and come closer each day.

> For me you're only a little boy just like a hundred thousand other little boys ... For you I'm only a fox

like a hundred thousand other foxes. But if you tame me, we'll need each other. You'll be the only boy in the world for me. I'll be the only fox in the world for you ...

It certainly sounds wonderful.

Playful as Foxes

YET ANOTHER MORNING at the crack of dawn. I'm driving away from home along the empty county road. Just after passing the traffic circle and the shop whose windows are still dark, I get a view across a field, and there in the middle stands a fox. It lifts its head and gazes skeptically at my car before taking off and vanishing into the edge of the forest as I dutifully return my eyes to the road. The parking lot is only a few hundred yards farther on. By the time I climb out of the car and raise my binoculars, the fox is already back in the middle of the field. It appears to have gotten caught up in some argument with the birds there because a crow and a gull are both lunging at it from the air, swooping low over the fox, which drops its head and ears. After a while, it seeks cover among the trees.

I cross the road. Before heading off onto a gravel track, I turn around and find the fox again with my binoculars. Now it too seems to want to cross the road. Sensibly, it looks right and left before crossing, but once it's reached the other side, a flock of gulls starts making a racket and the fox comes running back as fast as its legs will carry it, forcing a bus that's on its way across the plain to jam on the brakes and take evasive action to avoid running it over. Once again, the fox escapes into the forest and disappears.

The observation spot I've picked out lies a few stone's throws from the main road. I turn onto a trail alongside the bed of a forested brook, jump over the stream, and crash up through the undergrowth toward the edge of the field where I plan to sit. Here, I have a view across a different patch of field than the one I saw from the road. It slopes downward from where I'm standing, and down there on the other side of the field, a roebuck lies resting. He watches me rummaging around in the bushes and lifts his head, but apparently sees no reason to stand up. As soon as I quiet down, he seems to forget me.

This is new terrain that I have only just begun to explore. I don't know the foxes here. More precisely, I've previously caught a few glimpses of the one that narrowly escaped being run over by the bus—I knew it by the distinctively long white tip on its tail—and even before it appeared in the field, my plan had been to keep an eye out for that particular animal. I've been lucky. After barely an hour of waiting, the same fox shows up not far from the roebuck. Some small birds in a tree prompt the fox to rise up on its hind legs, forepaws on the tree trunk, and it stands like that for a while before giving up. Then it notices the roe deer. The buck has already stood up by the time the fox comes over to pick a fight—there's no other way of putting it. The fox makes little lunges at the buck, then jumps back to avoid his antlers. The buck gets irritated, of course, and apparently decides to chase off the fox once and for all, but it's no good—the fox is too quick as it ducks and dodges, and the buck simply finds himself tricked into a game that he clearly considers far beneath his dignity. Now and then, the fox sits down and looks the other way, at which point the roe deer tries to pretend nothing's going on either, but it isn't long before the fox starts harassing him again. The quarrel brings the two animals out into the field, in my direction. The slope up here isn't entirely even, so when they vanish out of sight in a hollow, I quickly put down my binoculars and fish out my camera. The fox comes running across the hillock, heading straight toward me, mouth half open, head and ears down, with the buck hot on its heels. Now they're pretty close. *Click, click.* The noise of the camera feels really loud and the roebuck seems uneasy—maybe he remembers there was someone up here earlier; at any rate, he stops and looks in the direction of the clicks, although he can't make me out in the shadows beneath the bushes. The fox keeps coming toward me. *Click, click, click.* Now both animals are wondering where the noise is coming from. The fox stops four or five yards

A curious red fox still shedding its winter coat.
Nesodden, Norway, May.

away from me, widens its eyes, and stares directly into the camera—puzzled, wild-eyed, utterly alert. Then it decides to continue onward into the forest to the right of me, but as I swing my long telephoto lens to follow it, it becomes aware of me at last and jumps backward. Then it gallops over to my other side, where it vanishes into the forest.

IF THERE'S ONE THING I'm left with after my efforts to get to know the red fox, it is this: the fox is a playful animal. It plays with its prey. It plays with objects.

It plays with parents and siblings, with its offspring, and sometimes with other members of its family group; it plays with potential partners before mating, and it even plays with an enemy like the roebuck. I have seen film clips of a wild red fox a few dozen miles from where I live that became the regular playmate of a German shepherd dog; another fox was filmed gate-crashing a game on a soccer field in Oslo and eventually running off with the ball; and in England, there was one fox that had collected a hundred pairs of stolen shoes. Of course, a wild animal can't play all the time. Sometimes the fox must fight for its life, flee from danger, or concentrate absolutely all its efforts on hunting, digging, or other necessary work. But play also seems to be important. Perhaps this is to do with the fox's adaptability, its versatile diet, and its flexible lifestyle. Because rather than enabling us to rehearse specific skills, it seems as if play helps us mammals to learn about ourselves and our surroundings, training us to handle unpredictable situations.

THE FOX'S METHOD is to try things out. It circles around the new, biting gently to see whether it will taste good or bite back. It leaps forward and beats an abrupt retreat, even if nothing happens. During the part of the day when it is out hunting or exploring, the fox is a hyperactive animal; it is lively, cautious, and curious. We could easily tell other stories about it; the fox has been firmly labeled as sly and cunning, but I think this is as much to do with the literature as the living creature. By all accounts, it's true that the fox is an intelligent animal. And it's hardly an accident that the most inventive and quick-witted species—foxes, crows, and ravens, say—are the ones that are depicted as tricksters rather than, for example, geese. But intelligence isn't just about cunning. When foxes manage to sneak into henhouses that the owners believe to be fox-proof—whether by digging, climbing, chewing through the wire mesh fence, or pushing down doors and hatches—it shows both ingenuity and determination, but these are hardly examples of cunning. The words "sly" and "cunning" refer to a particular form of intelligence that is aimed at other thinking beings; it revolves around the ability to get the better of or manipulate others by exploiting your insight into their motivations and views, while ensuring that *they* do not understand what you're up to until it is too late. The classic example of such behavior among foxes is that they apparently play dead to trick birds into coming close enough to be caught. This tale has been repeated countless times throughout history—by Bishop Olaus Magnus in the sixteenth century, among others. People certainly have seen this sequence of events. But maybe the fox was simply lying down dozing—and happened to be woken up by an inquisitive crow or magpie that was hoping to either nibble on a dead fox or tease a living one. Corvids, which often end up in conflict with the fox, are shrewd and playful creatures too.

Foxes probably do try to trick each other. Perhaps they sometimes think of ways to outfox people or other animal species too, for that matter. Intuitively, I'd think the fox is better at trickery than say, a badger or a roe deer; animals that hide food away for later and raid each other's food supplies the way foxes often do may find it useful to have a touch of slyness. The same is probably true of animals that constantly try hunting new kinds of prey, each with its own escape strategy. But when I think about the fox, cunning does not strike me as its most important characteristic. At any rate, Mikkel's/Reineke's/Reynard's ability to talk himself out of situations is a quality that is more pertinent to humans, loquacious and hyper-social creatures that we are. If we still recognize the flesh-and-blood animal in the tales of the cunning fox, that is because of his ingenuity, his boldness, and the fact that he finds a way out even when none seems possible. Mikkel's resourcefulness must be inspired by real, four-legged foxes.

ONE DAY AS I was walking along the forest trail looking for fox tracks, a memory came back to me that I hadn't recalled for many years. When I was a child, my mother would sometimes call me a fox. "You fox," she'd say. The next time I saw her, I asked where that idea had come from. It was kindly meant, she protested, and I remembered it that way too, as one of many affectionate nicknames. I don't know if it's relevant, but in the days when Mom used to call me a fox, I also had a tinge of the copper-red hair that had always been her own trademark. All this made me wonder whether something else lay beneath my interest in fox-watching, whether perhaps I identify with the fox at some level.

I don't feel especially wild, so that's hardly the explanation. But one reason I do feel a certain kinship with foxes is that they live together but hunt alone. Like most people, I need others around me—family, friends, and colleagues—but I'm also someone who needs time alone. I work best in solitude. I mostly pursue my leisure interests on my own, and nature seems to speak to me more clearly when there's no one with me keeping a conversation going.

For me, going out in search of foxes and discovering all the other creatures that live in forest and field is a project I pursue for the sheer pleasure of it—in other words, it's basically a form of play. It isn't particularly useful. Yet it makes me happy, and it feels meaningful in its way, as if this lets me live out my own particular version of human nature. After all, we are curious animals. As playful as foxes.

Thanks

NINA E. EIDE, senior research scientist at the Norwegian Institute for Nature Research, provided extensive comments on an early version of the manuscript. That was a great help. Gunnar Rogne and Hans Tjernshaugen read early drafts of chapters and offered useful comments. I'm also grateful for the advice from Mark Statham at the University of California, Davis, who reviewed the translated version and helped us add information relevant for North American readers.

I would like to thank those who have taken the time to help me approach the fox—whether the flesh-and-blood animal or the literary variety—in particular, Eystein Ruud in Nesodden, Helen Haanes in Oslo, Lona Holdt in Copenhagen, Miriam Mayer at the St. Anne's Museum in Lübeck, Stefan Funk at the Lübeck City Library, Irene Beyer at the Bjørneparken zoo in Flå, ethologist Anne Lene Hovland in Ås, and fur farmer Sigbjørn Kirkebøen in Hemsedal.

Additional thanks to all those who have answered questions and helped out with tips and other assistance, including Sigurd Aanderaa, Mikkel Berg-Nordlie, Line Marie Berteussen, Bård Bredesen,

Thomas Dam, Stephen Harris, Per Holck, Jørn Holm-Hansen, Alex Kacelnik, Oliver Kacelnik, Rune Karlsen, Marianne Løvstad, Arvid Olsen, Harald Røer, Håkon Strand, and Harald Weedon-Fekjær.

A big thank you to the Norwegian Non-Fiction Writers and Translators Association for a grant that enabled me to complete this book; to my employer at the time, the Great Norwegian Encyclopedia (snl.no), for allowing me to take a leave of absence so I could go fox-watching; to my Norwegian editor Joakim Botten, who helped me to find the right form; and to everyone at Kagge Forlag and Stilton Literary Agency.

During preparation of this English-language edition, I have very much enjoyed working with translator Lucy Moffatt and editor James Penco, as well as the rest of the team at Greystone Books.

Notes

Page v: "It is quite mad": English translation based on Lona
   Holdt's translation to modern Danish (2019, 65–66).

ON THE TRAIL

My main source here is Olsen (2012). I have also used Unwin
   (2015).

Page 9: "a little over half an inch thick": Information from Nina
   E. Eide, Norwegian Institute for Nature Research.

Page 10: "a newly opened jar of instant coffee": Hemmington
   (2014, 26–27).

LIKE CATS AND DOGS

The main sources for this chapter are Henry (1996, especially
   32–34 and 59–94); Macdonald (1987, especially 122–123);
   Macdonald et al. (2019); Macdonald and Sillero-Zubiri
   (2004); Bevanger (2012, 47–58); and Brand (2019, 17–21).
   The description of the genealogy of carnivorans and dogs is
   based on Wang and Tedford (2010) as well as Nyakatura and
   Bininda-Emonds (2012).

Page 15: "Pupils shaped like vertical slits occur mainly in": Banks
   et al. (2015).

Page 16: "clearly part of the same 'linguistic family'": Macdonald
   and Sillero-Zubiri (2004).

BLACKBACK

Drew (2017) was the starting point for some of the reflections here.

OF MICE AND VOLES

On the fox's diet in Scandinavia, I consulted Kjellander and Nordström (2003) and Panzacchi et al. (2008b). An important source for this chapter is Henry (1996).

WHY ROE DEER FEAR THE FOX

Important sources for this chapter include Andersen et al. (1998) [roe deer], Aanes and Andersen (1996), and Jarnemo and Liberg (2005) [the fox's predation of roe deer fawns], as well as Selås and Vik (2006), Smedshaug and Sonerud (1997), and Gervasi et al. (2012) [foxes, carnivorans, and deer in Norway].

Page 42: "When scientists . . . tagged newborn fawns with radio transmitters": Panzacchi et al. (2008a; 2008b; 2010).

Page 45: "the fox has lived up here in the north almost as long as humans": The oldest red fox finds in Norway are around 9,500 years old, according to Bevanger (2012, 47). As for humans, artifacts have been found from around 11,500 years ago and skeletons from around 9,000 years ago. See Persson (2019).

Page 46: "I once saw a recording from a wildlife camera": Rune Karlsen on Instagram, posted December 29, 2019.

TOWARD FALL

One of the main sources for this chapter is Macdonald (1987).

Page 49: "Swedish and Norwegian researchers who tagged red foxes with GPS transmitters": Walton et al. (2018).

Page 50: "several dozen square miles in barren environments": Bevanger (2012, 54–55) and Walton et al. (2017).

Page 50: "In British suburbs": Unwin (2015, 65–68), Baker et al. (2000, 135, figure 2), and Harris and Baker (2001).

FOXHUNT

Important written sources for this chapter are Hansen and Pedersen (2002), Kirkemo et al. (2003, 270–275), Weismann (1931), and several articles in a special issue edition of *Jeger* hunting magazine (Stenersen 2019; Winther 2019). A series of Norwegian Broadcasting Corporation programs that show differing forms of foxhunting also proved useful. For readers interested in the British foxhunting tradition and the conflict surrounding it, I recommend Jones (2017) and also Wallen (2006) for the older history.

Page 52: "Back in the Stone Age, people probably ate fox meat": Yeshurun et al. (2009).

Page 52: "It is only the meat of foxes and wolves that men reject": Magnus ([1555] 1998).

Page 53: "They prove an easy prey for crafty hunters": Magnus ([1555] 1998).

Page 53: "obtained these black pelts": It is unclear whether any black foxes lived in the Nordic region before silver foxes were imported from North America. See Frafjord (2022).

Page 55: "where there are fewer foxes, other small game is more abundant": See the chapter entitled "A Natural Experiment" in this book, as well as the accompanying notes.

Page 55: "One hunting magazine article cited an unnamed zoologist": Stenersen (2019).

Page 55: "long before the trapping takes place": Hansen and Pedersen (2002).

Page 58: "defend itself" and "Now it's time to get out spade and crowbar": Winther (2019).

TWENTIETH CENTURY FOXES

My main source here is Heger (2012) and, of course, Egner (1953)—as well as a later version of the audio play, and a printed edition from 2010, illustrated in color.

Page 61: "In the Chinese, Japanese, and Korean traditions": Wallen (2006, 60–71; 164–168).

Page 61: "which of the European languages is involved": The Croatian novel *Fox* (Ugresic 2018, 305) points out a link between the grammatical gender of the word in different languages and the gender the fairy-tale fox tends to be.

Page 61: "is called Elizaveta": Mikkel Berg-Nordlie, in personal communication with the author.

Page 63: "an era when edification was of the essence": This passage is inspired by Heger (2012, 297–309).

WHEN THE FOX PREACHES

Background sources include many of the contributions in Varty (2000), as well as Netterstrøm (2019), Svendrup (2017), Wallen (2006), Gibbs (2002), Menke (1992; 1998), Ziolkowski (1993), Terry (1983, introduction), Baltzer et al. (1928) [about Katarinenkirche], and Møller and Sandfeld (1923).

Page 65: "The philosopher Aristotle ... *Physiologus* ... Aesop's fables": Wallen (2006, 8–12; 45–46) and Ziolkowski (1993).

Page 65: "'That fox,' said Jesus of his enemy King Herod": Luke 13:32 (NIV).

Page 65: "encourages readers to do as the fox did": Gibbs (2002); Møller and Sandfeld (1923).

Page 67: "dating back to around 1335": Menke (1998).

Page 67: "in churches across much of Europe": Menke (1992, 19–26), Menke (1998, 3 and 5), Varty (2000, 145–148), and Svendrup (2017, 91–94).

Page 67: "the wolf in sheep's clothing": Referenced in Matthew 7:15 (NIV).

Page 68: "written in French, known as the *Roman de Renart*": Terry (1983), Wackers (2000), and Subrenat (2000).

Page 70: "The whole central character is a crook": Harty (2012, 139).

A FOX BOOK

The name Weigere is also spelled Veigere and Vejgere. For the Danish text, see Weigere (1555), Møller and Sandfeld (1915; 1923), and Holdt (2019). For those who prefer to read English, Simpson (2015) is a prose version of roughly the same story.

LONG NIGHTS

The main source for this chapter is Macdonald (1987).

Page 79: "parallel tracks of a pair of foxes walking together": Bevanger (2012, 49).

Page 79: "Their postures reveal an uneasy blend": Macdonald (1987, 212–213).

Page 80: "That may either be because they never came into heat": Macdonald (1987, 141) and Bakken (1993).

Page 81: "Yet genetic testing of foxes that lived": Baker et al. (2000) and Iossa et al. (2009).

Page 82: "In a short story called 'The Dogs in Thessaloniki'": Askildsen ([1996] 2021).

Page 82: "the prolonged coupling probably increases the likelihood": Unwin (2015, 51–52).

FEEDING TIME AT THE ZOO

In addition to the visit mentioned here, on February 17, 2020, when we were paying guests, I benefited greatly from a further visit to the Bjørneparken zoo outside opening hours, when the keeper, Irene Beyer, allowed me to meet the foxes and told me about her experiences with them.

Page 86: "Tembrock sketched and photographed in black-and-white more than sixty years ago": Tembrock (1957, 340, 450, 506).

THE MAN WITH THE FOXES

One of my main sources here is Kaspar and Wessel (2018). Tembrock (1957) is the source of most of the details about the foxes he kept, his work with them, and their behavior. Other important sources are Wessel (2008) and Wessel et al. (2013), in particular material from Kirsch (2008) and Tembrock (2008; 2013). Macdonald (2013) describes Tembrock's contributions to the field.

Page 87: "a letter to the more senior behavioral scientist Konrad Lorenz": Dated August 25, 1949, reproduced in an English translation in Tembrock (2013, 31).

Page 88: "Tembrock was ready to start publishing his findings": Tembrock (1957). Findings from the research were also discussed the previous year in Tembrock's book *Tierpsychologie* (Animal psychology), to which I have not had access (see Tembrock 2013).

Page 88: "Oof-oof"... and even "How-ow-ow-ow": Translated from the German original. Tembrock (1957, 396–409).

Page 88: "the Animal Sound Archive website": tierstimmenarchiv.de.

Page 88: "In the 1990s, some British researchers": Newton-Fisher et al. (1993).

Page 89: "are simply not among the fox's facial expressions": Macdonald and Sillero-Zubiri (2004, 7).

Page 90: "violet sniffing": Tembrock (1957, 338) ["*Violwittern*"]. For more about the glands, see Macdonald (1987, 125).

Page 91: "Sometimes, they perfume their feces": Macdonald (1987, 338).

Page 92: "Tembrock felt that he was being directly undermined": Tembrock (2013, 36–37); Kaspar and Wessel (2018, 26).

Page 93: "East Germans got to know him through a series of animal programs": Kaspar and Wessel (2018, 3).

Page 93: "the school of behavioral biology that Tembrock subscribed to": Even just meeting Western colleagues in his field may have been enough to make Tembrock an object of suspicion when the Cold War intensified in Berlin. The contact with Konrad Lorenz may have been a particular liability. Lorenz (unlike Tembrock and influential ethologists such as Nikolaas Tinbergen and Karl von Frisch) had been a member of Adolf Hitler's National Socialist Party and was a controversial figure in both East and West because some thought they detected a whiff of that background in his writings after the war too. See, for example, Klopfer (1994), which refers to such criticisms from the American behavioral scientist Daniel Lehrman in the 1950s. Author Rainer Kirsch mentions (to his mind, unfair) attacks on Lorenz in the East German press (2008).

Page 95: "Wulf Schiefenhövel delivered a blazing eulogy": The following paragraph is based on quotes from Schiefenhövel's eulogy, as reproduced in Kaspar and Wessel (2018), together with additional observations from those authors and from cultural researcher Sophia Gräfe in the same source.

Page 96: "species-typical behaviors": Tembrock (1957, 296).

A SUCCESSFUL SPECIES

Page 97: "hunting statistics": Statistics Norway (1978). In the record season of 1975–1976, roughly 67,000 animals were shot. Factors that influence hunting statistics other than fox populations are fur prices, bounties, and the number of hunters and their interest in foxhunting. See Smedshaug et al. (1999) and Selås and Vik (2006).

Page 98: "growth in deer populations ... disappearance of the large carnivorans": On the fox, carnivorans, and deer in Norway: Selås and Vik (2006), Smedshaug and Sonerud (1997), and Gervasi et al. (2012), as well as the chapter "Why Roe Deer Fear the Fox" in this book. The main view, that large carnivorans in Scandinavia and Finland (especially the wolf and the lynx) keep red fox numbers down when they are numerous, is confirmed by Elmhagen and Rushton (2007) and Elmhagen et al. (2010), although the research findings are not altogether unambiguous. A study carried out by Wikenros et al. (2017) in Sweden indicated that the presence of the lynx could, on the contrary, have a positive impact on fox populations, whereas the presence of the wolf appeared to reduce them, at least locally and over the short term.

Page 98: "There are several more factors that may help explain why": Jahren et al. (2020), Wikenros et al. (2017), Elmhagen and Rushton (2007), and Jarnemo and Liberg (2005).

THE COUSIN ON THE CRAGS

The Arctic fox, *Vulpes lagopus*, was previously considered to be a separate species known as *Alopex lagopus*.

Page 103: "may have been inhabited for millennia": Frafjord (2023).

Page 103: "If we're to believe Günter Tembrock": Tembrock (1960).

Page 105: "mostly found along highways and near holiday cabins": Rød-Eriksen et al. (2020) and Selås et al. (2010).

Page 105: "boom-and-bust cycle of the lemming population": Angerbjörn et al. (2013); Ims et al. (2017).

Page 105: "A warmer climate also means": Ims et al. (2017), Elmhagen et al. (2015; 2017), and Hickler et al. (2012).

Page 106: "around fifty adult animals": Angerbjörn et al. (2013) [Forty to sixty adult animals in 2000].

Page 106: "roughly three hundred adult Arctic foxes": Eide et al. (2020).

Page 106: "biologists have managed to reestablish the Arctic fox": Landa et al. (2017).

QUARANTINE

The passage about fox tapeworm is based on information from the websites of the Norwegian Food Safety Authority and the Norwegian Veterinary Institute, as well as the Norwegian Institute of Public Health guidelines. The section about rabies and the history of the disease in Europe is largely based on material in King et al. (2004).

Page 108: "GPS tagging of red foxes has revealed": Walton et al. (2018).

Page 108: "they often cross national borders": Skår (2017).

Page 108: "a legal text on clay tablets . . . dating back nearly four thousand years": Yuhong (2001, 33).

Page 109: "the teeth and gums of the upper jaw": Swabe (2004, 316).
Page 109: "In 1580... red foxes were said to": Blancou (2004, 19).
Page 110: "A major new rabies outbreak": Müller et al. (2004)
and Pastoret et al. (2004).
Page 111: "attempt a large-scale vaccination campaign": Steck et
al. (1982) and Aubert et al. (2004, 141–142).

A NATURAL EXPERIMENT

Davidson et al. (2008) and Mörner (1992) offer an overview of
mange and the epidemic in the Nordic region.
Strains of scabies that specialize in attacking humans, foxes, and
other mammals, respectively, are considered to be different
variants of the same species. In English, the human disease is
known as "scabies," whereas infection with scabies mites in all
other animal species is called "mange."
Page 113: "best be compared with the Black Death": The Black
Death and subsequent outbreaks of the plague are thought to
have reduced the population of Norway by an estimated
60 percent over a period of 150 years.
Page 113: "Fox numbers plummeted by well over half": Smedshaug
et al. (1999, 158). The population reduction for Sweden is estimated at more than 70 percent; see Lindström et al. (1994).
Page 114: "Grimsö Wildlife Research Station": Lindström et al.
(1994).
Page 115: "Roe deer also had more luck": Kjellander and Nordström (2003).
Page 115: "Hunting statistics showed that more hares": Smedshaug et al. (1999).
Page 116: "Foxes... and the scabies mite reached a kind of uneasy
equilibrium": Davidson et al. (2008) and Carricondo-Sanchez
et al. (2017).

UNDERGROUND

The main sources for this chapter are Alvarez-Betancourt
(2016), an appearance by Alvarez-Betancourt on an episode

of *The Nature of Things* called "Fox Tales" (2017), Harris and Baker (2001, 49–50), Bevanger (2012, 52–53), and Unwin (2015, 49–63).

Page 119: "You can find videos of fox births on the internet": Video clips from foxes' dens in a Dutch national park uploaded to YouTube by the Dutch Forest Service, among others, at: youtube.com/watch?v=ss1yoI4LEwo and youtube.com/watch?v=vWqrfsAmwKo. These clips also form part of Alvarez-Betancourt's source material (see above note).

Page 120: "Fox mothers that were observed in captivity": Braastad (1993).

Page 121: "foxes don't help their young by regurgitating half-digested food": Several popular science books claim that foxes regurgitate food for their young. However, if you consult scientists who have studied the reproductive behavior of dogs and other canids in detail, they explain that this method is not seen among red foxes and that it occurs more or less exclusively on the wolf's side of the canid family. See Macdonald and Sillero-Zobiri (2004) and Macdonald et al. (2019).

A DEN OF THIEVES

Page 127: "fight over food with 'astonishing savagery'": Macdonald (1987, 45).

Page 131: "David Macdonald reports one case in which a subordinate vixen": Macdonald (1987, 145), summarized in Macdonald and Sillero-Zubiri (2004, 96).

Page 139: "Some suggest setting up a seat or other observation platform": Pedersen (1956, 11–34).

URBAN FOXES

Page 141: "The foxes are pushy because they get fed": Strømme (2020).

Page 144: "In Bristol, southwest England, urban foxes": Baker et al. (2000), Harris and Baker (2001), and Iossa et al. (2009).

Page 144: "urban foxes are middle-class": Harris and Baker (2001, 100).

Page 145: "a very small part of the diet": Harris and Baker (2001, 71).

Page 145: "warmly recommends feeding foxes": Harris and Baker (2001, 78).

Page 146: "In a TV documentary from 2017": "Fox Tales" (2017).

Page 146: "Bristol's local authorities, however, advise against feeding": Bristol City Council (n.d.).

Page 146: "there have been a few cases of foxes biting": Jones (2017, 236–241).

Page 146: "As Stephen Harris says": Winterman (2013).

FARMED FOXES

The main written sources here are official documents: *Norsk pelsdyrhold—bærekraftig utvikling eller styrt avvikling?* [Norwegian fur farming—sustainable development or managed wind-down?] (2014); *Meld. St. 8 (2016–2017) Melding til Stortinget, Pelsdyrnæringen* [Parliamentary report (2016–2017), Fur-farming industry] Ministry of Agriculture and Food (2016); as well as Hovland et al. (2017), Prichard (1926), and Storsul (2001). The official documents reproduce responses to public consultations, which reveal different parties' views of fur farming. I also benefited from a conversation with former fur animal researcher, Anne Lene Hovland. The provision on the winding-down of the industry is contained in an act of Parliament passed on June 21, 2019.

Page 149: "from a Canadian breeder for $10,000": Norges sølvrevavlslag [Norwegian silver fox breeders association] (1936, 58) ("$10,000 or roughly kr. 37,000 delivered to the farm in Canada").

Page 149: "More livestock was also imported from Canada": Both to Norway and other countries, see Prichard (1926) and Trut et al. (2020).

Page 151: "a fundamental need to form part of social groups": Rådet for dyreetikk [Council for Animal Ethics] (1994).

Page 152: "breeders were supposed to try to make fur animals tamer": *Norsk pelsdyrhold* (2014, 50). The requirement to breed more trusting animals was later tightened further; see overview in Ministry of Agriculture and Food (2016, 39–42).

Page 160: "judged the welfare of the farm foxes to be 'adequate'": Akre et al. (2008, 5).

Page 161: "domestication has shaped them ... that is to say, their genetic makeup": The word "domestication" is sometimes used like this and sometimes in such a way that it covers both the genetic changes over generations and the taming of each individual animal through habituation.

Page 162: "retained the entire behavioral repertoire ... less 'reactive,'": Hovland et al. (2017, 256); conversation with Anne Lene Hovland.

PET FOXES

The main sources here are Dugatkin and Trut (2017) and Trut (1999) [the Belyaev experiment], as well as Hare (2017) and Wrangham (2019) [the hypothesis of human self-domestication]. The name Belyaev is sometimes rendered as "Belyayev" in English.

Page 164: "My life is monotonous": Saint-Exupéry ([1943] 2013, 60–61).

Page 165: "One friend sent me a black-and-white photo": Sigurd Aanderaa, personal communication.

Page 165: "won Instagram fame as Ayla the Fox": Grøtte and Matnisdal (2017).

Page 166: "alternative view of the relationship between evolution, nature, and nurture": This relates, in particular, to Trofim Lysenko; see, for example, Graham (2016) and Roll-Hansen (2004).

Page 169: "Experts in the field still debate how many similarities": Lord et al. (2020a; 2020b), Zeder (2020), and Trut et al. (2020).

Page 171: "human self-domestication hypothesis": Hare (2017).

Page 171: "talent for interpreting people's pointing and gaze": Hare et al. (2005).

Page 173: "People with experience of keeping foxes as pets": Jones (2017, 79). Lovely depictions of life with domesticated foxes (born wild) can be found here and in Macdonald (1987).

Page 174: "One fox owner speaks of the time": Wagner (2017).

Page 174: "It would have been better to return at the same time": Saint-Exupéry ([1943] 2013, 60–61).

Page 174: "For me you're only a little boy": Saint-Exupéry ([1943] 2013, 58).

PLAYFUL AS FOXES

The sources for play among mammals in general are Graham and Burghardt (2010) and Drew (2017).

Page 181: "it's hardly an accident": Netterstrøm (2019).

Page 181: "maybe the fox was simply lying down dozing": Harris and Baker (2001, 39 and 134).

References

Aanes, Ronny, and Reidar Andersen. 1996. "The effects of sex, time of birth, and habitat on the vulnerability of roe deer fawns to red fox predation." *Canadian Journal of Zoology* 74, no. 10 (October): 1857–1865.

Akre, Anne Kathrine, et al. 2008. *Risk Assessment Concerning the Welfare of Animals Kept for Fur Production.* Report to the Norwegian Scientific Committee for Food Safety (VKM).

Alvarez-Betancourt, Sandra. 2016. "Juvenile behavioural development and intra-litter hierarchy establishment in captive red fox cubs (*Vulpes vulpes*)." Unpublished PhD thesis, University of Bristol.

Andersen, Reidar, et al., eds. 1998. *The European Roe Deer: The Biology of Success.* Oslo: Scandinavian University Press.

Angerbjörn, Anders, et al. 2013. "Carnivore conservation in practice: Replicated management actions on a large spatial scale." *Journal of Applied Ecology* 50, no. 1 (February): 59–67.

Askildsen, Kjell. (1996) 2021. "The Dogs of Thessaloniki." In *Everything Like Before: Stories by Kjell Askildsen*, translated by Seán Kinsella, 119–128. New York: Archipelago Books.

Aubert, M. F., et al. 2004. "Rabies in France, the Netherlands, Belgium, Luxembourg and Switzerland." In *Historical Perspective of Rabies in Europe and the Mediterranean Basin*, edited by Arthur A. King et al., 129–145. Paris: OIE.

Baker, Philip J., et al. 2000. "Flexible spatial organization of urban foxes, *Vulpes vulpes*, before and during an outbreak of sarcoptic mange." *Animal Behaviour* 59, no. 1 (January): 127–146.

Bakken, M. 1993. "The relationship between competition capacity and reproduction in farmed silver-fox vixens, *Vulpes vulpes*." *Journal of Animal Breeding and Genetics* 110, no. 1–6 (January–December): 147–155.

Baltzer, Johan, et al. 1928. *Die Bau-Und Kunstdenkmäler der Freien Hansestadt Lübeck* (The architectural and artistic monuments of the Free Hanseatic City of Lübeck), volume IV. Lübeck: Verlag von Bernhard Nöhring.

Banks, Martin S., et al. 2015. "Why do animal eyes have pupils of different shapes?" *Science Advances* 1, no. 7 (August): e1500391.

Bevanger, Kjetil. 2012. *Norske rovdyr* (Norwegian predators). Oslo: Cappelen Damm.

Blancou, J. 2004. "Rabies in Europe and the Mediterranean Basin: From antiquity to the 19th century." In *Historical Perspective of Rabies in Europe and the Mediterranean Basin*, edited by Arthur A. King et al., 15–24. Paris: OIE.

Brand, Adele. 2019. *The Hidden World of the Fox*. New York: HarperCollins.

Braastad, Bjarne O. 1993. "Periparturient behaviour of successfully reproducing farmed silver-fox vixens." *Applied Animal Behaviour Science* 37, no. 2 (July): 125–138.

Breisjøberget, Jo Inge, et al. 2018. "The alternative prey hypothesis revisited: Still valid for willow ptarmigan population dynamics." *PloS One* 13, no. 6 (June): e0197289.

Bristol City Council. n.d. "Urban foxes." Accessed October 14, 2020. bristol.gov.uk/pests-pollution-noise-food/urban-foxes.

Carricondo-Sanchez, D., et al. 2017. "The range of the mange: Spatiotemporal patterns of sarcoptic mange in red foxes (*Vulpes vulpes*) as revealed by camera trapping." *PloS One* 12, no. 4 (April): e0176200.

Davidson, Rebecca K., et al. 2008. "Long-term study of *Sarcoptes scabiei* infection in Norwegian red foxes (*Vulpes vulpes*) indicating host/parasite adaptation." *Veterinary Parasitology* 156, no. 3–4 (October): 277–283.

Davidson, Rebecca K., et al. 2009. "*Echinococcus multilocularis*—adaptation of a worm egg isolation procedure coupled with a multiplex PCR assay to carry out large-scale screening of red foxes (*Vulpes vulpes*) in Norway." *Parasitology Research* 104, no. 3 (February): 509–514.

Drew, Liam. 2017. *I, Mammal: The Story of What Makes Us Mammals.* London: Bloomsbury Sigma.

Dugatkin, Lee Alan, and Lyudmila Trut. 2017. *How to Tame a Fox (and Build a Dog): Visionary Scientists and a Siberian Tale of Jump-Started Evolution.* Chicago: University of Chicago Press.

Egner, Thorbjørn. 1953. *Klatremus og de andre dyrene i Hakkebakkeskogen* (Climbing Mouse and the other animals of the Huckybucky Forest). Oslo: Cappelen.

Egner, Thorbjørn. 2010. *Klatremus og de andre dyrene i Hakkebakkeskogen* (Climbing Mouse and the other animals of the Huckybucky Forest). 17th edition. Oslo: Cappelen Damm.

Eide, Nina E., et al. 2020. *Fjellrev i Norge 2020. Resultater fra det nasjonale overvåkingsprogrammet for fjellrev* (The Arctic fox in Norway 2020. Results from the national monitoring program for Arctic foxes). Research report. Trondheim: Norwegian Institute for Nature Research (NINA).

Elmhagen, Bodil, and Stephen P. Rushton. 2007. "Trophic control of mesopredators in terrestrial ecosystems: Top-down or bottom-up?" *Ecology Letters* 10, no. 3 (March): 197–206.

Elmhagen, Bodil, et al. 2010. "Top predators, mesopredators and their prey: Interference ecosystems along bioclimatic productivity gradients." *Journal of Animal Ecology* 79, no. 4 (July): 785–794.

Elmhagen, Bodil, et al. 2015. "A boreal invasion in response to climate change? Range shifts and community effects in the borderland between forest and tundra." *Ambio* 44, suppl. 1 (January): 39–50.

Elmhagen, Bodil, et al. 2017. "Homage to Hersteinsson and Macdonald: Climate warming and resource subsidies cause red fox range expansion and Arctic fox decline." *Polar Research* 36, suppl. 1.

"Fox Tales." 2017. *The Nature of Things*, season 56, episode 18. Directed by Susan Fleming and Roderick Deogrades. Originally aired on March 23.

Frafjord, Karl. 2022. "Svartrev" (Black fox). Store norske leksikon (Great Norwegian Encyclopedia). Last updated February 1, 2022. snl.no/svartrev.

Frafjord, Karl. 2023. "Fjellrev" (Arctic fox). Store norske leksikon (Great Norwegian Encyclopedia). Last updated July 19, 2023. snl.no/fjellrev.

Gervasi, V., et al. 2012. "Predicting the potential demographic impact of predators on their prey: A comparative analysis of two carnivore–ungulate systems in Scandinavia." *Journal of Animal Ecology* 81, no. 2 (March): 443–454.

Gibbs, Laura. 2002. Introduction and notes to *Aesop's Fables*, by Aesop, translated by Laura Gibbs. Oxford: Oxford University Press.

Graham, Kerrie Lewis, and Gordon M. Burghardt. 2010. "Current perspectives on the biological study of play: Signs of progress." *Quarterly Review of Biology* 85, no. 4 (December): 393–418.

Graham, Loren. 2016. *Lysenko's Ghost: Epigenetics and Russia*. Cambridge, MA: Harvard University Press.

Grøtte, Leiv Magnus, and Silje Elin Matnisdal. 2017. *Ayla the Fox. Reven som sjarmerte en hel verden* (Ayla the fox: The fox who charmed a whole world). Bryne: Jæren Forlag.

Hansen, Henning, and Helge B. Pedersen. 2002. *Jakt og fangst av rødrev* (Hunting and trapping the red fox). Pamphlet published by Norges Jeger- og Fiskerforbund (Norwegian Association of Hunters and Anglers).

Hare, Brian, et al. 2005. "Social cognitive evolution in captive foxes is a correlated by-product of experimental domestication." *Current Biology* 15, no. 3 (February): 226–230.

Hare, Brian. 2017. "Survival of the friendliest: *Homo sapiens* evolved via selection for prosociality." *Annual Review of Psychology* 68 (January): 155–186.

Harris, Stephen, and Phil Baker. 2001. *Urban Foxes.* 2nd edition. Essex: Whittet Books.

Harty, Kevin J. 2012. "Walt in Sherwood, or the sheriff of Disneyland: Disney and the film legend of Robin Hood." In *The Disney Middle Ages: A Fairy-Tale and Fantasy Past*, edited by Tison Pugh and Susan Aronstein, 133–152 (New York: Palgrave Macmillan).

Heger, Anders. 2012. *Egner. En norsk dannelseshistorie* (The life and works of Thorbjørn Egner). Oslo: Cappelen Damm.

Hemmington, Martin. 2014. *Fox Watching: In the Shadow of the Fox.* 2nd edition. Essex: Whittet Books.

Henry, J. David. 1996. *Red Fox: The Catlike Canine.* 2nd edition. Washington: Smithsonian Institute Press.

Hickler, Thomas, et al. 2012. "Projecting the future distribution of European potential natural vegetation zones with a generalized, tree species-based dynamic vegetation model." *Global Ecology and Biogeography* 21, no. 1 (January): 50–63.

Holdt, Lona. 2019. *En rævebog* (A fox book). Copenhagen: Multivers. Rendered in modern Danish from Herman Weigere's 1555 translation of *En Raeffue Bog*.

Hovland, Anne Lene, et al. 2017. "Behaviour of foxes and mink kept for fur production." In *The Ethology of Domestic Animals: An Introduction*, edited by Per Jensen, 255–270 (Wallingford: CABI).

Ims, Rolf A., et al. 2017. "Ecosystem drivers of an Arctic fox population at the western fringe of the Eurasian Arctic." *Polar Research* 36, suppl. 1 (August): polarresearch.net/index.php/polar/article/view/2716.

Iossa, G., et al. 2009. "Behavioral changes associated with a population density decline in the facultatively social red fox." *Behavioral Ecology* 20, no. 2 (March): 385–395.

Jahren, Torfinn, et al. 2020. "The impact of human land use and landscape productivity on population dynamics of red fox in southeastern Norway." *Mammal Research* 65, no. 3 (April): 503–516.

Jarnemo, Anders, and Olof Liberg. 2005. "Red fox removal and roe deer fawn survival: A fourteen-year study." *Journal of Wildlife Management* 69, no. 3 (July): 1090–1098.

Jones, Lucy. 2017. *Foxes Unearthed: A Story of Love and Loathing in Modern Britain*. London: Elliott & Thompson.

Kaspar, Frank, and Andreas Wessel. 2018. *Tembrocks Tierleben* (Tembrock's animal life). Script of a radio documentary first broadcast on June 3. Available at swr.de.

King, Arthur A., et al., eds. 2004. *Historical Perspective of Rabies in Europe and the Mediterranean Basin*. Paris: OIE.

Kirkemo, Ole, et al., ed. 2003. *Aschehoug og Gyldendals jakt, fiske og friluftsliv i Norge. Bind 1: Lavland* (Aschehoug and Gyldendal's hunting, fishing, and outdoors life in Norway. Volume 1: Lowlands). Oslo: Kunnskapsforlaget.

Kirsch, Rainer. 2008. "Der Verhaltensforscher Professor Tembrock" (The behavioral scientist, professor Tembrock). In *"Ohne Bekenntnis keine Erkenntnis,"* edited by Andreas Wessel, 121–143. Bielefeld: Kleine Verlag.

Kjellander, Petter, and Jonas Nordström. 2003. "Cyclic voles, prey switching in red fox, and roe deer dynamics—a test of the alternative prey hypothesis." *Oikos* 101, no. 2 (May): 338–344.

Klopfer, Peter. 1994. "Konrad Lorenz and the National Socialists: On the politics of ethology." *International Journal of Comparative Psychology* 7, no. 4: 202–208.

Landa, Arild, et al. 2017. "The endangered Arctic fox in Norway—the failure and success of captive breeding and reintroduction." *Polar Research* 36, suppl. 1 (September): polarresearch.net/index.php/polar/article/view/2723.

Lindström, Erik R., et al. 1994. "Disease reveals the predator: Sarcoptic mange, red fox predation, and prey populations." *Ecology* 75, no. 4 (June): 1042–1049.

Lord, Kathryn, et al. 2020a. "The history of farm foxes undermines the animal domestication syndrome." *Trends in Ecology & Evolution* 35, no. 2 (February): 125–136.

Lord, Kathryn, et al. 2020b. "Reply to Zeder and Trut et al.: An attractive hypothesis in need of evidence." *Trends in Ecology & Evolution* 35, no. 8 (June): 651–652.

Macdonald, David W. 1987. *Running With the Fox*. London: Unwin Hyman.

Macdonald, David W. 2013. "From ethology to biodiversity: Case studies of wildlife conservation." In *Quo Vadis, Behavioural Biology? Past, Present, and Future of an Evolving Science*, edited by Andreas Wessel et al., 111–156. Halle: Germany Academy of Natural Scientists Leopoldina.

Macdonald, David W., and Claudio Sillero-Zubiri, eds. 2004. *The Biology and Conservation of Wild Canids*. Oxford: Oxford University Press.

Macdonald, David W., et al. 2019. "Monogamy: Cause, consequence or corollary of success in wild canids?" *Frontiers in Ecology and Evolution* 7 (June): doi.org/10.3389/fevo.2019.00341.

Magnus, Olaus. (1555) 1998. *A Description of the Northern Peoples*, volume III, edited by Peter Foote and translated by Peter Fisher and Humphrey Higgens. London: Hakluyt Society.

Mann, Jill. 2000. "The satiric fiction of the *Ysengrimus*." In *Reynard the Fox: Social Engagement and Cultural Metamorphoses in the Beast Epic From the Middle Ages to the Present*, edited by Kenneth Varty, 1–16. New York: Berghahn Books.

Ministry of Agriculture and Food. 2016. *Meld. St. 8 (2016–2017) Melding til Stortinget, Pelsdyrnæringen* (Parliamentary report [2016–2017], Fur-farming industry). regjeringen.no/no/dokumenter/meld.-st.-8-20162017/id2518504/.

Menke, Hubertus. 1992. *Bibliotheca Reinardiana. Teil 1: Die europäischen Reineke-Fuchs-Drucke bis zum Jahre 1800* (Bibliotheca Reinardiana: Part 1: European print editions of Reineke Fox until the year 1800). Stuttgart: Hauswedell.

Menke, Hubertus. 1998. *Die Unheilige Weltbibel. Der Lübecker Reynke de Vos (1498–1998)* (The unholy world bible: Reynke de Vos of Lübeck (1498–1998)). Abteilung für niederdeutsche Sprache und Literatur der Christian-Albrechts-Universität zu Kiel. Exhibition program.

Møller, Niels, and Kristian Sandfeld, eds. 1915. *En Raeffue Bog* (A fox book), vol. 1. Copenhagen: Det danske Sprog -og Litteraturselskab. [Reproduces the contents of Herman Weigere's 1555 book, with explanations and commentaries in Danish.]

Møller, Niels, and Kristian Sandfeld, eds. 1923. *En Raeffue Bog* (A fox book), vol. 11. Copenhagen: Det danske Sprog -og Litteraturselskab. [Reproduces the contents of Herman Weigere's 1555 book, with explanations and commentaries in Danish.]

Mörner, T. 1992. "Sarcoptic mange in Swedish wildlife." *Revue Scientifique et Technique (Office International des Epizooties)* 11, no. 4 (December): 1115–1121.

Müller, W., et al. 2004. "Rabies in Germany, Denmark and Austria." In *Historical Perspective of Rabies in Europe and the Mediterranean Basin*, edited by Arthur A. King et al, 79–89. 2004. Paris: OIE.

Netterstrøm, Jeppe Büchert. 2019. "Ræv i galge" (Fox on the gallows). *Temp–Tidsskrift for historie* 9, no. 17 (January): 133–137.

Newton-Fisher, Nicholas E., et al. 1993. "Structure and function of red fox *Vulpes vulpes* vocalisations." *Bioacoustics* 5 (January): 1–31.

Nordhagen, R. 1950. "Mikkelsbær, mikkelsfisk og Mikkel rev. Sjødemonen og djevelen" (Foxberries, foxfish and Mikkel Rev: The seadevil and the devil). Yearbook. Bergen: University of Bergen.

Norges sølvrevavlslag. 1936. *Norges sølvrevavlslag 1926–1936. Jubileumsskrift* (Norwegian silver fox breeders association 1926–1936, anniversary publication).

Norsk pelsdyrhold—bærekraftig utvikling eller styrt avvikling? Gjennomgang av pelsdyrnæringen (Norwegian fur farming— sustainable development or managed wind-down? Review of the fur-farming industry). 2014. *NOU 2014:15.* Norges offentlige utredninger. regjeringen.no/no/dokumenter/nou-2014-15/id2353568/.

Nyakatura, Katrin, and Olaf R.P. Bininda-Emonds. 2012. "Updating the evolutionary history of Carnivora (Mammalia): A new species-level supertree complete with divergence time estimates." *BMC Biology* 10, no. 12 (February): doi.org/10.1186/1741-7007-10-12.

Olsen, Lars-Henrik. 2012. *Sportegn fra dyr* (Animal tracks). Oslo: Aschehoug.

Panzacchi, Manuela, et al. 2008a. "When a generalist becomes a specialist: Patterns of red fox predation on roe deer fawns under contrasting conditions." *Canadian Journal of Zoology* 86, no. 2 (February): 116–126.

Panzacchi, Manuela, et al. 2008b. "Evaluation of the importance of roe deer fawns in the spring–summer diet of red foxes in southeastern Norway." *Ecological Research* 23, no. 5 (September): 889–896.

Panzacchi, Manuela, et al. 2010. "Trade-offs between maternal foraging and fawn predation risk in an income breeder." *Behavioral Ecology and Sociobiology* 64, no. 8 (April): 1267–1278.

Pastoret, P. P., et al. 2004. "European rabies control and its history." In *Historical Perspective of Rabies in Europe and the Mediterranean Basin*, edited by Arthur A. King et al., 337–347. Paris: OIE.

Pedersen, Alwin. 1956. *Fribyttere og kongeligt vildt* (Buccaneers and royal game). Copenhagen: J. Fr. Clausens.

Persson, Per Åke. 2019. "De første menneskene i Norge" (The first people in Norway). Norgeshistorie, University of Oslo, April 3, norgeshistorie.no/eldre-steinalder/0116-def%C3%B8rste-menneskene-i-norge.html.

Prichard, James H. 1926. *The Silver Fox in Captivity*. Summerside, PEI: Canadian Silver Fox Breeders' Association.

Rådet for dyreetikk (Council for Animal Ethics). 1994. "Pelsdyroppdrett" (Fur farming). Oppnevnt av Landbruks- og matdepartementet (Appointed by the Ministry of Agriculture and Food). Statement issued in October. Accessed November 9, 2020. radetfordyreetikk.no/pelsdyroppdrett/.

Rasmussen, Tarald. 2017. "En grunnfortelling om reformasjonen i Tyskland" (A master narrative of the Reformation in Germany), in *Reformasjonen i nytt lys* (The Reformation in a new light), edited by Tarald Rasmussen and Ola Tjørhom, 11–46. Oslo: Cappelen Damm.

Rød-Eriksen, L., et al. 2020. "Highways associated with expansion of boreal scavengers into the alpine tundra of Fennoscandia." *Journal of Applied Ecology* 57, no. 9 (September): 1861–1870.

Roll-Hansen, Nils. 2004. *The Lysenko Effect: The Politics of Science*. Amherst, NY: Humanity Books.

Saint-Exupéry, Antoine de. (1943) 2013. *The Little Prince*, translated by Richard Howard. Boston: Houghton Mifflin Harcourt.

Selås, Vidar, and J. O. Vik. 2006. "Possible impact of snow depth and ungulate carcasses on red fox (*Vulpes vulpes*) populations in Norway, 1897–1976." *Journal of Zoology* 269, no. 3 (July): 299–308.

Selås, Vidar, et al. 2010. "Arctic fox *Vulpes lagopus* den use in relation to altitude and human infrastructure." *Wildlife Biology* 16, no. 1 (March): 107–112.

Simpson, James, trans. 2015. *Reynard the Fox: A New Translation*. New York: Liveright.

Skår, Frode. 2017. "Rødrevens vandring forbløffer forskerne"
(Scientists surprised by the travels of the red fox). forskning.no,
May 29, forskning.no/dyreverden-partner-hogskolen-i-
innlandet/rodrevens-vandring-forbloffer-forskerne/344399.

Smedshaug, Christian A., and Geir A. Sonerud. 1997. "Rovdyr,
åtsler og predasjon på småvilt" (Predators, scavengers, and
predation on small game). *Fagnytt naturforvaltning* 4, no. 8
(October): 1–4.

Smedshaug, Christian A., et al. 1999. "The effect of a natural
reduction of red fox *Vulpes vulpes* on small game hunting bags
in Norway." *Wildlife Biology* 5, no. 3 (September): 157–166.

Statistics Norway. 1978. *Jaktstatistikk 1846–1977* (Hunting statistics: 1846–1977).

Steck, F., et al. 1982. "Oral immunisation of foxes against rabies:
A field study." *Zentralblatt für Veterinärmedizin Reihe B* 29,
no. 5 (June): 372–396.

Stenersen, Jo. 2019. "Revejakt som viltstell: Revnende likegyldig
for reven?" (Foxhunting as game management: A matter of the
greatest indifference to the fox). *Jeger* no. 2, 2019.

Storsul, Einar. 2001. *Pelsdyrnæringa i fokus. Norges Pelsdyralslag
gjennom 75 år, 1926–2001* (The fur-farming industry in focus:
The Norwegian Fur Farming Association over 75 years,
1926–2001).

Strømme, Edvin. 2020. "Revene fra Malmøya tar seg til rette i
båter: – Hylte da jeg våknet med den ved siden av meg" (The
foxes of Malmøya make themselves at home in boats: Howled
when I woke up with it beside me). *Nordstrands Blad*, June 25.

Subrenat, Jean. 2000. "Rape and adultery: Reflected facets of
feudal justice in the *Roman de Renart*." In *Reynard the Fox:
Cultural Metamorphoses and Social Engagement in the Beast
Epic From the Middle Ages to the Present*, edited by Kenneth
Varty, 17–36. New York: Berghahn Books.

Svendrup, Torben. 2017. *Når ræven vogter gæs: Reformationen i
de danske kalkmalerier* (When the fox guards the geese: The

Reformation in the Danish frescoes). Copenhagen: Kristeligt Dagblads Forlag.

Swabe, J. 2004. "Folklore, perceptions, science and rabies prevention and control." In *Historical Perspective of Rabies in Europe and the Mediterranean Basin*, edited by Arthur A. King et al., 311–322. Paris: OIE.

Tembrock, Günter. 1957. "Zur Ethologie des Rotfuchses (*Vulpes vulpes* [L.]), unter besonderer Berücksichtigung der Fortpflanzung" (Toward an ethology of the red fox (*Vulpes vulpes* [L.]), with particular regard to reproduction). *Der Zoologischen Garten* 23, no. 4–6 (January): 289–532.

Tembrock, Günter. 1960. "Spielverhalten und Vergleichende Ethologie. Beobachtungen zum Spiel von *Alopex lagopus* (L.)" (Play behavior and comparative ethology: Observations on the play of *Alopex lagopus* (L.)). *Mammalian Biology* 25 (January): 1–14.

Tembrock, Günter. 1963. "Mischlaute beim rotfuchs (*Vulpes vulpes* L.)" (Mixed vocalizations in the red fox (*Vulpes vulpes* L.)). *Ethology* 20, no. 5 (March): 616–623.

Tembrock, Günter. 2008. "70 Jahre Humboldt-Universität" (70 years at Humboldt University). In *"Ohne Bekenntnis keine Erkenntnis,"* edited by Andreas Wessel, 25–28. Bielefeld: Kleine Verlag.

Tembrock, Günter. 2013. "Change of concepts of behavior over the last 60 years at Humboldt University Berlin." In *Quo Vadis, Behavioural Biology? Past, Present, and Future of an Evolving Science*, edited by Andreas Wessel et al., 29–60. Halle: Germany Academy of Natural Scientists Leopoldina.

Terry, Patricia, trans. 1983. *Renard the Fox*. Boston: Northeastern University Press. [Translation of *Roman de Renart* from Old French to English.]

Trut, Lyudmila. 1999. "Early canid domestication: The farm-fox experiment." *American Scientist* 87 (March): 160–169.

Trut, Lyudmila, et al. 2020. "Belyaev's and PEI's foxes: A far cry." *Trends in Ecology & Evolution* 35, no. 8 (August): 649–651.

Ugresic, Dubravka. 2018. *Fox*, translated by Ellen Elias-Bursać and David Williams. Rochester, NY: Open Letter.

Unwin, Mike. 2015. *Foxes*. RSPB Spotlight series. London: Bloomsbury.

Varty, Kenneth, ed. 2000. *Reynard the Fox: Cultural Metamorphoses and Social Engagement in the Beast Epic From the Middle Ages to the Present*. New York: Berghahn Books.

Wackers, Paul. 2000. "Medieval French and Dutch Renardian epics: Between literature and society." In *Reynard the Fox: Cultural Metamorphoses and Social Engagement in the Beast Epic From the Middle Ages to the Present*, edited by Kenneth Varty, 55–72. New York: Berghahn Books.

Wagner, Andrew. 2017. "Why domesticated foxes are genetically fascinating (and terrible pets)," *PBS Newshour*, March 31, 2017, pbs.org/newshour/science/domesticated-foxes-genetically-fascinating-terrible-pets.

Wallen, Martin. 2006. *Fox*. London: Reaktion Books.

Walton, Zea, et al. 2017. "Variation in home range size of red foxes *Vulpes vulpes* along a gradient of productivity and human landscape alteration." *PloS One* 12, no. 4 (April): e0175291.

Walton, Zea, et al. 2018. "Long-distance dispersal in red foxes *Vulpes vulpes* revealed by GPS tracking." *European Journal of Wildlife Research* 64 (October): doi.org/10.1007/s10344-018-1223-9.

Wang, Xiaoming, and Richard H. Tedford. 2010. *Dogs: Their Fossil Relatives & Evolutionary History*. New York: Columbia University Press.

Weigere, Herman. 1555. *En Raeffue Bog* (A fox book). Available online at the website of the National Library of Norway.

Weismann, Carl. 1931. *Vildtets og jagtens historie i Danmark* (The history of game and hunting in Denmark). Copenhagen: Reitzel.

Wessel, Andreas, ed. 2008. *"Ohne Bekenntnis keine Erkenntnis." Günter Tembrock zu Ehren* (Festschrift in honor of Günter Tembrock). Bielefeld: Kleine Verlag.

Wessel, Andreas, et al., eds. 2013. *Quo Vadis, Behavioural Biology? Past, Present, and Future of an Evolving Science. International Symposium of the Humboldt-Universität zu Berlin and the German National Academy of Sciences Leopoldina*. Halle: Germany Academy of Natural Scientists Leopoldina.

Wikenros, Camilla, et al. 2017. "Fear or food—abundance of red fox in relation to occurrence of lynx and wolf." *Scientific Reports* 7, no. 1 (August): doi.org/10.1038/s41598-017-08927-6.

Winterman, Denise. 2013. "Outfoxing the urban fox." *BBC News Magazine*, October 22: bbc.com/news/magazine-24563919.

Winther, Arne. 2019. "Den store revejakta: Reveknep mot revestreker" (The great foxhunt: Foxy tricks to outfox the fox). *Jeger* no. 2.

Wrangham, Richard. 2019. *The Goodness Paradox. How Evolution Made Us Both More and Less Violent*. London: Profile Books.

Yeshurun, Reuven, et al. 2009. "The role of foxes in the Natufian economy." *Before Farming* 1 (January): 1–15.

Yuhong, Wu. 2001. "Rabies and rabid dogs in Sumerian and Akkadian literature." *Journal of the American Oriental Society* 121, no. 1 (January): 32–43.

Zeder, Melinda A. 2020. "Straw foxes: Domestication syndrome evaluation comes up short." *Trends in Ecology & Evolution* 35, no. 8 (August): 647–649.

Ziolkowski, Jan M. 1993. *Talking Animals: Medieval Latin Beast Poetry, 750–1150*. Philadelphia: University of Pennsylvania Press.